Lava Orange

Buards Red

CHRISTOPHORUS EDITION

“It is the pinnacle of achievement to create something that survives the test of time, is immune to the eccentricity of certain epochs - in other words, has a timeless character.”

Prof. Dr. Ing h.c. Ferry Porsche

Gentian Blue Metallic

Jörg Walz

#99x911

The history of the Porsche 911

DELIUS KLASING VERLAG

#Preface

#It has arrived. The rebirth of a legend. The eighth of its kind. The new Porsche 911. Generation 992. More muscular. More powerful. More sustainable. Distinctive. It lifts the pure feeling of driving, digitalized, into a new era. A true high-performance car. The best Porsche of all time. Once again. Proof of the right path into the future; tradition and innovation going hand in hand. The 911 is ahead of its time. At the same time, it is committed to its origins. And an invitation to reflect on a few keywords.

#Generations.

A symbol of shared origins. The passing down of genes is the basis of all life. Along the way, they learn to adapt and change. All life strives to make progress, confronting challenges and overcoming change. Children carry on the values of their parents into a new era, and yet are defiantly individual at the same time. They are given existence, after which they forge ahead as unique individuals. Yet they will always be defined by where they have come from. Every Porsche 911 is a descendant of the original. Since 1963, it has been the worthy successor of the 356, the first sports car to bear the name 'Porsche.' All subsequent generations, although unmistakably heirs to the throne, have also been shaped by their respective times. Thus every 911 becomes the guardian of its own history. But there is one thing common to them all: they are all carrying on the legend.

#Timelessness.

Time is marked by a beginning and end. Natural limits. Within that, there is room to act. Products are victims of nature. Myths are not. It's hardly surprising, then, that the art of escaping the unchangeable is appreciated. One strength of the Porsche 911 is its ability to provide trailblazing solutions to the needs of the moment. It is true, however, that the individual car is at the mercy of time, although it is worth noting that more than 70% of all Porsches ever built are still being run today. And, even if they are not being driven, the memories, the feelings and stories that are attached to the 911 are always alive. They are timeless.

#Icons. Success. Contrasts.

Images. In ancient Greek: eikón. Icons. True, convincing representations of abstract thoughts, intangible constructs and feelings. "Icon 911" — a bit over the top, some might think. Misuse of a historical cultural heritage, sleazy marketing, unabashed self-congratulation, flagrant lack of all subtlety. But what drives our customers? What leads them to spend their money on a car? Success, independence and freedom, fine engineering, striving for something better. A powerful need for forward progress, for perfection. Dissatisfaction with mediocrity. The combination of exclusivity and social acceptance, restraint and discipline. It is the contrasts that make the myth of the 911 a passion. The credo of historical mission and uncompromising progress: Icon 911.

#Feeling.

Feeling for a car. What sounds like the beginning of a mediocre joke based on stereotypes is actually reality. Getting a feel for a car begins with how you feel inside it; driving a Porsche 911 is an escape from the outside world. Time seems to flow. Everyday drudgeries begin to fade away. The 911's practical functionality is enhanced by its beauty and quality. It is the epitome of a sports car — a luxury product and a work of art.

#Commitment.

Every 911 is the best in the company's history. What may appear to be criticism of the eighth generation 911's unquestionable resemblance to previous iterations is actually a testament to the work and skill of the car's designers. Recognizable features from earlier models are a nod to past triumphs. The roots of success remain. When developing its vehicles, Porsche always makes the distinction between things that are time-honoured and things that are simply obsolete. Never be afraid to change and adapt, however radically.

But preserve what's worth keeping. Retain what's inspiring. This school of thought is not one of mindless conservatism; reliable and timeless technology will always manage to fend off new developments. Evolution instead of revolution. This is Zuffenhausen's mission statement.

What began in 1963 with the birth of the 911 finds — once again — its ultimate form. And yet is never finished.

Dr. Josef Arweck

#In sequence

#A marvelous model

The 911 is an iconic sports car without parallel. Throughout its more than five decades, it has not merely grown along with the demands of its customers and environment — but in fact has consistently shifted the horizons and defined the limits of possibility. This has enabled the 911 to be both remarkably mature yet fresh at the same time. The Porsche 911 is the epitome of the German sports car. As such, it has been a highly prized top import from the start. It is a dream car, admired and coveted while at the same time appreciated almost without envy. A self-employed 911 owner can visit customers without sparking excessive envy. And while sports cars from other makers usually bear a grim expression, the 911 has always worn a friendly smile. Added to this is the interplay of forms, with virtually perfect proportions and desirable curves.

The 911 functions as a vintage antique, as a classic car, as a used car or as a new car. The price of the 6-cylinder boxer sports car ranges from that of a factory-new compact car to the price to buy a yacht or luxury property.

And a 911 is more versatile than any other sports car. It copes without a murmur or complaint with the demands of daily life — and of course with „occasional use as a leisure vehicle or sports car."

The 911 is available as a thoroughbred racing car or can range from a rather minimalist sports car to an opulently equipped luxury car. Power is supplied to the rear wheels — with plenty of traction — or to all four wheels — with even more traction. Power is always supplied by a 6-cylinder boxer engine, originally one with two liters of displacement. The volume of the combustion chamber in the most powerful 911 engine is twice this size. Its standard engine power output, intended for road traffic, ranges from 110 hp to a phenomenal 700 hp. The 911 comes with an aspirated engine or a supercharged engine. As a "turbo," the sports car from Zuffenhausen has made turbocharging technology fashionable and brought it to maturity. It has long since become the standard for today's environmentally friendly, efficient and low-emission combustion engines.

The 911 has a streamlined body and is contoured with curves of various widths. The body always fits like a perfectly tailored sheath. Each generation of the 911 redefines the standard of beauty. Regardless of the model line, a 911 is always attractive — visually and otherwise. And without making its predecessor suddenly look old. A 911 is always sex appeal in automotive form.

The various body versions also add to the versatility of the 911: as a Coupé, a targa or a Cabriolet. And the sports car that originated in 1963 as the sole model and meanwhile has been available in three versions — the 911 SC, targa and turbo — has long since become a model series with two dozen different model variants, not including special limited series products. At the same time, the extensive list of selectable options and the equipping of each vehicle with individual and unique details and colors offers unprecedented possibilities for customization.

As a result, the 911 can seem thoroughly contradictory. Yet it is a straightforward, uncompromising, loyal companion. And has been for more than five decades. In eight generations. More than one million units produced and coveted billions of times over. And incidentally, not only at full scale but also in miniature — as a scaled-down replica that reproduces almost every variation of the 911 theme, true to scale. In this spirit, I hope you enjoy browsing, looking at, reading about and journeying through the history of the marvelous one: the 911.

Jörg Walz

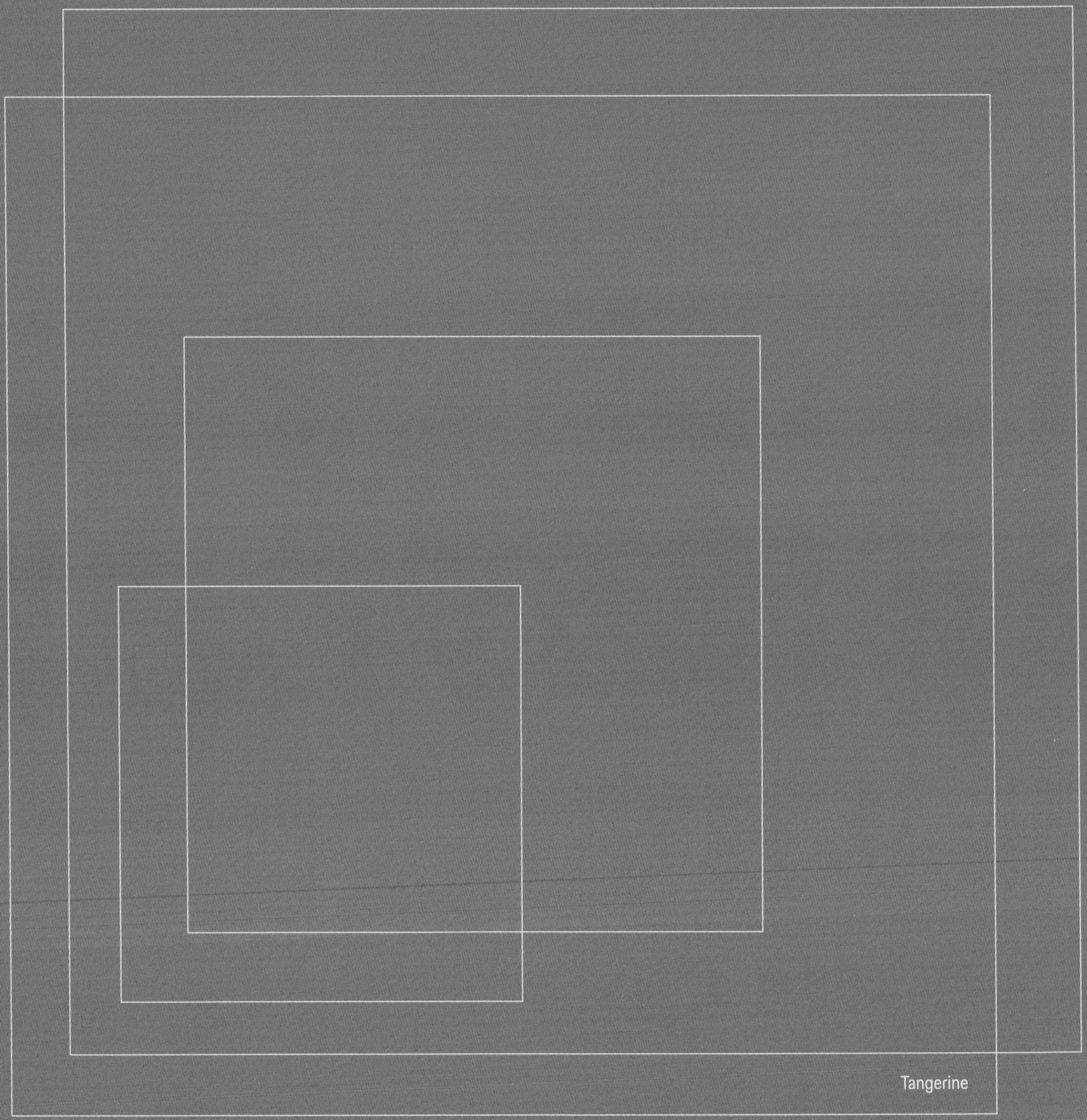
Tangerine

#Generation I

(901 and 911)

Porsche T8 901 “bat” prototype, 1962
Masterpiece of automotive culture; Obermembach, Bavaria

Olive Green

#The Erl King

#New cars can generally do everything better than their predecessors, which makes the predecessor look old from one day to the next. So it is easy to understand why car manufacturers are always careful to present their new creations to the public only when they are ready for the market and for production. And since the product creation process requires a substantial amount of time, including an extensive test phase on public roads, the industry traditionally cloaks and conceals its prototypes with bulky attachments, adhesive films and other means of camouflage. These cloaked prototypes are colloquially called "Erl Kings" by Germans. This is loosely based on the poem of the same name by Johann Wolfgang von Goethe: "Who's riding so late through the endless wild?..."

In a kind of game played between car manufacturers and car magazines, the media have for decades used drawings and computer representations to decipher photographs of camouflaged prototypes. This is usually to the annoyance of the carmakers, who still need to deliver the current predecessor model to their customers. **But sometimes the situation is different, as was the case of the Erl King photos that were leaked to the media in the run-up to the IAA Frankfurt in 1963. They showed a new sports car from Stuttgart — appearing slightly out of focus and therefore authentic.** They were not captured by an Erl King photographer, but instead were intentionally staged on a road between Weilimdorf and Münchingen, not far from Weissach, the future headquarters of the Porsche development center. With these photos, the Porsche press chief at the time, Fritz Huschke von Hanstein, drew attention to the successor to the aging 356, and secured prominent coverage of the car that would be one of the stars of the Frankfurt Motor Show in late summer 1963. This was a way to arouse the curiosity of potential customers.

The originally white Erl King, hastily and carelessly painted over in matte green, featured an air intake on the front hood, covered side windows at the rear, a central support over the rear window, and a rear attachment spanning the fenders and hood with two large fins, which made its profile view appear sedan-like. This hid the original contours of the eventual production vehicle from curious eyes. **The two wing-like fins also gave the prototype its nickname: "bat." This was the second of a full dozen prototypes that Porsche produced for the 901.** Testing and development drives began in autumn 1962. The prototypes were continuously modified and ultimately went the way of almost every prototype: At the end of 1964, the bat was also scrapped. Series production of the new 6-cylinder sports car began at that point — after some delay. Porsche spent around 15 million marks on its development and acquired the Reutter body shop in Stuttgart for an additional 6 million marks. The considerable investments were also a cause for concern, however, as the future of the young sports car brand was riding on the success of "the newcomer." The success of its decades-long career and millions of units sold could not be foreseen in the mid-1960s.

Porsche 901/911, 1963
Minichamps; Wolfenbüttel

Champagne Yellow

#And they're off and running!

#Stuttgart was already thinking about a successor to the 356 by the second half of the 1950s. But the company was small, the production numbers were still low and the costs for developing a new car were high. It would take until the end of the decade for the 901 or 911 project to take concrete shape — and at that time, there was no discussion of the 911. The projects that were to lead to a modern four-seater vehicle went by the numbers 695 and 754. In 1961, Ferry Porsche, son of design genius Ferdinand Porsche and founder of the post-war sports car brand, specified that the new model should have a wheelbase of 2.20 meters, 20 centimeters shorter than originally planned. This meant the concept of a four-seater was off the table. Two-plus-two would have to suffice. **"Others can do four seats better," Ferry Porsche is quoted as saying.** A new engine with six cylinders and two cooling air blowers was being built under the project code 745. Starting in 1963, young engineer and Porsche grandson Ferdinand K. Piëch began helping navigate the way out of this dead end. The result was a new air-cooled 2.0-liter 6-cylinder boxer with the name 821. However, because the engine was not yet finished in September 1963, the champagne yellow vehicle for the IAA exhibition was left with a gaping hole. The car for the fair was a stationary model. Yet this did not dampen visitor enthusiasm — even if the new Porsche did not meet with unanimous approval. The focus of criticism, aside from the price, was on the shape of the car. This was based on the 356 but was still completely new. "The austere shape was daring at the time, in part because many people were still attached to the shape of the 356," Wolfgang Porsche recalled. His father Ferry Porsche swiftly responded to the critics: "When you like something tre-mendously from the start, it doesn't last." The lines bore the signature of Ferry's son Ferdinand Alexander Porsche, nick-named "Butzi." The design was created in 1961. **In the first sales brochure, the company described the 901 as "solid workmanship of tasteful materials on a virtually handcrafted basis."** In fact, the new 6-cylinder sports car was being pro-duced in homeopathic doses. And it was late, since pilot production first began in spring 1964. Porsche was finally able to deliver the first production car on October 27. The last of a total of 82 Porsche 901s would be completed in mid-November. The 6-cylinder-2+2 was then delivered as the 911. At the end of the calendar year, Porsche's books showed only 232 units of the 911 had been produced. And the company was also not able to achieve the price that Porsche had mentioned at the IAA. Instead of the DM 23,900 initially announced, the price was reduced by DM 2,000 at the launch of series production. It was a rocky start.

#Green is the color of hope.

#Ferry Porsche, it was said, preferred a lush green color for his company car, like the Irish Green that covered the 901 of the head of the company. The market introduction of the new model was preceded by an exchange of letters between Sochaux, France — the location of the Peugeot headquarters — and Stuttgart-Zuffenhausen. Peugeot asked Porsche to refrain from using the type designation 901, since it has been a tradition of the brand with the lion in its signet since 1929 to designate its vehicles with three-digit numbers, all of which carry a 0 in the middle. Interestingly, the French appeared to have first gotten around to making this request in autumn 1964, after the debut of the Porsche at the Paris Salon. The new sports car with the name 901 apparently continued to fly under the radar at the IAA. As a result, the 901 became the 911 and the 4-cylinder sibling model originally christened the 902 became the 912.

Even before Porsche showed consideration for the request from Peugeot, the strategists in Stuttgart had cast an eye toward Wolfsburg — more specifically toward the sales, service and spare parts organization that Porsche had always shared with Volkswagen. **In the early days of the computer age, numbering systems had begun to play a role.** These systems could be used to catalog spare parts and organize the associated logistics. And in the much more extensive cosmos of the Volkswagen numbering system, there happened to be space free in the still unclaimed 900 series of digits. Thus the newcomer became the 901, and then the 911.

But more important than its name was its performance data: 130 hp was a bold declaration. The 6-cylinder engine thus stood out from the crowd of mid-'60s automobiles, which ranged from the Cabin Scooter, the Beetle and Kadett to the Kapitän and S-Class models. With its 1,991 cc of displacement, this translated to a power density of 65 hp. The body, compared to that of the 356, was 4 cm flatter and 20 cm longer, embodying the sportiness that more than did justice to the top speed of 210 km/h. "To make unrestricted use of the lightning-fast acceleration of the powerful 6-cylinder engine, in which the experiences from Grand Prix engine development were exploited, the 911 was fitted with a new, fully synchronized 5-speed transmission with patented, internationally proven Porsche ring synchronization," the brochure stated at the time. **And lightning-fast meant that the 911 could sprint from a standstill to 100 km/h in 9.1 seconds.** The country road speed limit did not yet exist in those days, meaning Germany's roads outside towns remained free of speed limits.

In terms of driving dynamics, the early vehicles still needed to be taught some manners: Directional stability was lousy and the tail-heavy Coupé turned out to be sensitive to side winds. The result of tuning efforts was a more sensitive, precisely adjusted chassis with controlled, prestressed torsion bars on the front axle and 22 kg of ballast in the bumper ends. **This made the 911 predictable and drivable for people outside the Porsche development department as well.**

Irish Green

Porsche 901, 1964
Minimax; Herzogenaurach

#The 911 conquers the world

#At the start of 1965, Porsche was producing five 911s a day in Zuffenhausen. The test drivers who had already been allowed to drive the 911 were enthusiastic. "Automobil Revue," for example, reported: "The new Porsche follows the line of the highly sporty but comfortable touring car." Another Porsche press release would definitely be considered politically incorrect today: "Expert testers all over the world have repeatedly used the word 'bomb' to describe the 6-cylinder 911. And bombs are created more for 'tough guys' than for women." This made one thing clear: The 911 was masculine — a far cry from the 60 hp version of the 356 known as the "Lady."

Porsche had paved its way into the world with the 356. **The trailblazer was Max Hoffman, who emigrated to the United States from Austria. He made the European car brands big in America and thereby amassed a small fortune.** Porsche was also initially part of Hoffman's portfolio — starting in 1969, Porsche was distributed in the United States by Volkswagen. Sales through Hoffman — a genius salesman who is credited as the catalyst for cars like the Mercedes 300 SL, BMW 507 Roadster, Alfa Romeo Giulietta Spider and Porsche 356 Speedster — were preceded by a conversation with Ferry Porsche, who in the 1950s said to Hoffman: "I will be satisfied if you sell five cars a year." Hoffman's response: "If it's not at least five a week, I'm not interested." The US developed into Porsche's most important and largest market. In 1967, one out of every two Porsches went to the United States.

In 1965, the 911 was one of the most modern vehicles in the world. Details like a seatbelt preparation system, laminated-glass windshield, electric windshield wiper system with three speeds and a twelve-volt vehicle electrical system were trappings that were not yet standard in those days. This was also true for the five-speed transmission. The first gear was at the left rear. This allowed quick and smooth shifting between the second and third gear, which were the most-used gears on racetracks and country roads. The hands gripped a steering wheel rim made of wood — like the dashboard panel, which extended across the width of the car. The car rolled on 165 tires with a 15-inch format. Compared to the early 901, the unladen weight of what was still a 130-hp 911 grew from 1,000 to 1,080 kg. **From 1964 to 1967, 10,723 units of the 911 2.0 had already been produced...**

White

Porsche 911 (original model), 1965
Welly; Brooklyn

Porsche 912, 1965
Schuco Junior Line; Porsche Museum Stuttgart

Ossi Blue

#Sweetening the start

#... by 1969 Porsche had produced a full 32,867 units of the 912 that appeared in 1965. After production of the 356 had ceased, there was a customer group for whom the leap to the 6-cylinder was too great. From the start, the Porsche sales team had been committed to bridging the gap between the 356 and the 901. The launch of the 902 project dated back to 1962.

In April 1965, the price list for the newly created 912 — a 911 body with a 356 1.6-liter 4-cylinder engine at the rear and scaled-back equipment — showed DM 16,250. The 902 and 912 could be selected with a 4- or 5-speed transmission. The price climbed in August to DM 17,600 but dropped two years later, in August 1967, to DM 17,000. The reason was the introduction at that time of the 911 T, which for a mere DM 2,000 more, made it possible to enter the world of the 6-cylinder engine. This ultimately meant the days of the 912 were numbered. However, the limited production period for the 912 had been planned from the start. But prior to that, the 912 had been the right model at the right time. It secured turnover and returns for Porsche during a time of transition and financially intensive expansion. The 90-hp 4-cylinder engine found numerous fans, primarily in the US market.

The 912 weighed 1,010 kilograms — while the 356 B 1600 Super 90, with an identical engine, weighed 60 kg less. Nevertheless, the 912 cut the time for the sprint from 0 to 100 km/h by half a second, with 13.5 seconds. And at 183 km/h, it is a hair faster than the shorter 356 (180 km/h). The 912 also had no need to shy away from comparison with the 130-hp 6-cylinder engine, as its engine weighed 54 kilograms less, giving the 4-cylinder rear-engined sports car a pleasant balance and unexpected agility. **In 1966, the first full year of production, Porsche sold three times as many 912s as its 6-cylinder sibling model.** Incidentally, the 100,000th Porsche was a 911 — a targa — in Pure White. Porsche gave it away on December 21, 1966 — practically as an early Christmas present — to the police, who at the time relied on Porsche even more heavily as a supplier of patrol cars. The final death knell for the 912 with a 356 engine finally sounded in 1969. The reason was California's environmental requirements, which had meanwhile become much more stringent and were no longer achievable with the aging 4-cylinder engine. A revision would have been much too expensive. And if the harmonious 911 T, pared down to essentials, was too expensive, starting in 1969 you could choose a new 4-cylinder alternative: the VW Porsche 914.

In 1975 Porsche once again offered a 912. The 912 E got the 2.0-liter engine from the Porsche 914 or VW 412. This model was reserved exclusively for US customers. **But with the 924, which appeared in the mid-1970s, Porsche added an equally self-contained and attractive sports car to the lower end of the model range.** So the 912 E only got to dance for one summer, since after only 2,092 vehicles being built, it was over.

#Open to innovation

#Porsche produced the first 911 with a sunroof in June 1965. But that was not enough for American Porsche dealers. They missed having a convertible version of the 911, since up to then, open-top sports cars had been an integral part of the model range. Not least because of the high interest from the US market, Porsche showed the open-top version of the 911, the targa, at the IAA 1965. A "safety convertible" that fit well with the safety-related discussion at the time. The explosive spread of the automobile in the mid-1960s was accompanied by negative developments such as air pollution and an increasing number of victims of traffic accidents. Porsche found a charming solution with the relatively harmonious integration of the roll bar into the design of the car — and at the same time solved issues with body stiffness that made it difficult to modify the early 911 into a convertible.

The name targa fit Porsche in two ways: for one, the word "Targa" means "protective shield" in Italian and, for another, it is the name of the Sicilian road race of the same name: the Targa Florio, in which Porsche was competing year after year against Alfa Romeo and Ferrari for sporting domination.

The appearance of the stainless steel roll bar initially took some getting used to — as has so often been the case throughout the history of Porsche, there were vocal critics at the start. Even the in-house magazine *Christophorus* mockingly asked whether household detergent should be used to clean it. But Porsche was making a statement with the roll bar that would ultimately be copied by other sports car manufacturers. **The rear window in the early targa was made of plastic and could be opened with a zipper.** This made the targa versatile: Porsche called the closed version "Hardtop," the version with an open folding roof "Voyager," that with an open rear window and closed roof "Bel-Air," and the completely open version "Spyder." This poetic bit of marketing did not catch on with the general public, but that did not hurt the success of the targa. It found its fans from the start and, as a result, was worth producing in significant numbers. The surcharge for the version of the 911 with a softer, more torsional body was initially DM 1,400 and rose, starting in 1970, to DM 2,220. That was about 10 percent of the base price of a 911 T.

Signal Orange

Porsche 911 targa "Soft Window," 1965
Schuco Junior Line; Würzburg

#Boost in performance

#Porsche had found an entry point for its customers with the 912. With the 911 S, released in 1966, the sports car manufacturer found more power in its quest for performance. **With a vigorous 160 hp, the new top model was able to achieve a speed of 220 km/h. This made the 911 S Germany's fastest production car.** The 2.0-liter 6-cylinder engine mobilized its rated output at 6,600 crankshaft revolutions per minute, but the engine could also handle 7,200 rpm. These were impressive values for a racing engine at that time, far from the 5,200 rpm of a 356 C 1600 C, or the fabulous 6,200 rpm of the 356 C 2000 GS Carrera 2. The standard performance of the 2.0-liter 911-S increased from the 1969 model year to 170 hp — thanks to an oil cooler, fuel injection and other engine-related measures. When the 1970 model year appeared one year later, in late summer 1969, 180 horses were already working — thanks to the larger 2.2 liters of displacement — under the flat, sloping hood of the sports car that could now achieve 225 km/h. Aficionados recognized it in their rear-view mirror primarily due to the chrome-plated fog lights mounted below the bumper. The standard 911 still rolled on the rather narrow 165/15 tire size favored by Ferry Porsche, but the wheels are now made of forged light alloy. The design — like that of the car — comes from the hand of "Butzi" Porsche. **Fuchs is the name of the manufacturer of the aluminum wheel that has become characteristic over the decades.** Starting in 1968, the rim and tire width were allowed to grow. The new dream dimension became 185, which at the time was considered a wide tire. Hidden behind them were the internally ventilated disc brakes — the first of their kind in an automobile. And the occupants of the car would note the leather-covered steering wheel. Only mechanics would get to see the adjustable shock absorbers, the new stabilizer on the rear axle and the ventilated disc brakes on the front axle.

Porsche works driver Vic Elford became the European Rally Champion in 1967 with a 911 S Rally. He is not the only competitor to succumb to the charms of the 911. "Porsche hp count for double," Walter Röhrl once stated, adding the explanation: "The 180 hp in the Porsche 911 S were then simply there. Without losses. Not like the Abruzzo ponies, but rather with real horsepower — thanks to the rear engine without a cardan shaft but with superb power transmission. Given the same output as other cars, even the early Porsche always had more power." Like so many others before and since, the rally virtuoso — called a "genius on wheels" by Formula 1 champion Niki Lauda — succumbed to the magic of the 911. "There is no other car that transfers the power as directly to the asphalt as the 911 does. Regardless of whether I move the steering wheel, accelerate or apply the brakes — in the 911, I always have direct contact with the road. A Porsche drives precisely where I steer it. Completely unfiltered." But the 911 is also considered a challenge: "Especially at the upper limit, because there it demands sensitivity and your undivided attention. Otherwise, you will quickly become the passenger."

Canary Yellow

Porsche 911 S, 1966
Norev; Irgertsheim

Porsche 911 R, 1967
Kyosho; Berlin

Polo Red

#Let's see what it can do

#While the 911 S by then denoted the pinnacle of the 911 series, Porsche developers — first and foremost among them the young Ferdinand K. Piëch — were trying to gage the maximum and to measure it during sporting events. **From the start, the 6-cylinder also competed in races and rallies, including the Monte Carlo Rally, in which the young Porsche employee and later race director Peter Falk competed in 1965 with aplomb in a 911 powered up to 160 hp.** Traditionally, however, it has been experienced race drivers and sporty individuals who have driven a Porsche to the starting line in countless other races. Porsche supports its active customers with cars further developed especially for this purpose. Alongside the relatively unknown 911 S 2.0 "Rallye," the 911 R 2.0 presented to the trade press in Hockenheim in 1967 was an especially hot topic of discussion. Its "pointy" engine with eightfold mounted, forged crankshaft, double ignition, two triple carburetor and dry sump lubrication originated from the flat, 98-centimeter-high "Carrera 6" 906 racing car prototype, but is slowed by 10 hp to 210 hp. The weight of the R, which is limited to 20 vehicles, was likewise reduced. Developers had melted no less than 280 kilograms off of the series production vehicles. **This was made possible by the use of plastic hoods and doors, panes of thin Plexiglas, and other, consistent weight reduction measures, including smaller rear lights.** The result of this meticulous effort was an unladen weight of 800 kilograms. Almost too much of a good thing: the plastic front hood was so thin that it was deformed by the airflow produced during driving. The 911 R became immortalized through its record runs in Monza, during which more than 20,000 kilometers unreeled in one go despite the unpleasant late autumn weather. And at an average speed of 209 km/h.

Due to its low quantities, the 911 R remained a prototype in formal legal terms from a sport regulations perspective. And here, its prototype cousins in the caliber of a 906, 907 or 910 were of more advantageous stature. A minimum series of 500 units was required for homologation to series GT, but Porsche Sales did not see any sales opportunities for them. **It's not hard to understand: the 911 R, at DM 45,000, cost almost twice as much as the 911 S, at DM 24,500.**

#In 1967 Porsche extended the model range of the 911 with the 911 T. **T stands for "Touring" and a great way to get your foot in the door with a 6-cylinder engine reduced to 110 hp.** That was still enough for a respectable top speed at that time of 200 km/h. The power reduction was achieved by reducing combustion chamber compression compared to the more powerful model. Just 5,800 rpm was also enough for the 6-cylinder engine to mobilize maximum power. An automatic transmission entered the stage as an additional comfort feature. The reason for this could once again be found in the USA, where studies showed a generation growing up in the local market without having learned how to handle a clutch pedal. Porsche knew how to help itself: **With the help of the supplier Sachs, the sports car manufacturer developed its so-called "Sportomatic."** Strictly speaking, this was a semi-automatic transmission that eliminated the clutch pedal, but the driver still had to select the gears. A servo motor disconnected the clutch as soon as the driver touched the gear shift for the 4-speed transmission. Extra charge: DM 990. Purists shook their heads. They also didn't care for the five kilograms of added weight and the five km/h reduction in top speed.

Porsche tried to give the new automatic a sporty look by participating with the Sportomatic 911 in the Marathon de la Route, an 84-hour endurance race at the Nürburgring (the predecessor of the legendary 24-hour race on the Nordschleife). Jochen Neerpasch and Vic Elford completed this mission with a victory. The irony of the story: The automatic version has ultimately proved more popular in Europe than across the pond.
The previous 911 with 130 hp received a new designation, specifically, the appendage L for "luxury." In the sum of its parts, the 911 is a well-rounded package that consisted of exactly 9,675 individual parts — that, at least, was what was written in the sales literature at the time.

A further concession to the requirements of the New World was the notable introduction of an emission control system, which Porsche would be offering from late summer of this year. And without any loss of performance. California's mandatory emission control was a must for Porsche, since the company depended largely on US exports for its livelihood.

#Harmonious and well-mannered

Leaf Green

Porsche 911 T, 1967
WhiteBox; Tennenloher Forst

#It can sometimes be difficult to keep track of when a model is produced over many years and in numerous variants. Porsche has therefore always kept records. For example, the original 911 with the short wheelbase (and without any model name appendages) runs as a zero series in Porsche's in-house number records — not to be confused with the pre-series. The so-called A-series, produced from 1967 to '68, follows in its footsteps. For customers, the 911 now comes with the designations T, S and L.

The 1969 model year, manufactured between August 1968 and July 1969, is referred to internally by Porsche as the B Series. The most notable feature is the extension of the wheelbase from 2,211 to 2,268 millimeters. Slight cantilever extensions on the fenders make room for larger wheels. The L becomes the E. Now with 140 hp. And the output of the 911 S increases to 170 hp.

The gas mixture is now prepared by means of electric fuel injection instead of the carburetor system. At that time Porsche was discussing the necessity of a successor model. However, the high investments for development and preparations for production of a new model were counterbalanced by the still modest quantities of the dream sports car.

In 1970 Porsche produced 73 units of the 911 per day in Zuffenhausen. Two thirds as Coupés, one third as targas.

By the 1970 model year, the displacement had grown to 2.2 liters before increasing further to 2.4 liters by the 1972 model year change. **Internally, the 2.2-liter 911s are counted in the C and D series.** The thirst of the 2.2-liter engines corresponds to that of its predecessors with smaller displacement, but thanks to somewhat increased torque, the new engines are more elastic and smoother in their power delivery. When high-octane fuel then began to face criticism from Americans, Porsche reacted by approving regular gasoline. German drivers couldn't believe their eyes: regular gasoline was sufficient for the ultimate sports car? Porsche increased displacement to 2.4 liters. Record-keepers in Stuttgart include these years in the E and F series. **The G-model follows starting in August 1973 (with the model year 1974). This is primarily noticeable in the new bumper bellows — another response to demands from overseas.** But that is yet another story.

#On the way to becoming an evergreen

Light Ivory

Porsche 911 L, 1968
Minichamps; Hockenheimring

#Urban outlaw

#Long, shaggy hair, an equally unkempt beard, usually wearing sturdy shoes and a rather conspicuous hat — these are the trademarks of Magnus Walker, who likes to call himself an "urban outlaw." And Walker is indeed breaking with convention. His career has brought the British Porsche fan to the United States through exchange programs and ultimately to Los Angeles. Through revamped second-hand fashion he has managed to become an entrepreneur in textiles with his own label, a small production facility in a loft that has repeatedly attracted the interest of filmmakers, and a unique Porsche collection. Unique because none of his cars are in standard condition. Each of his Porsches bears the signature of Magnus Walker. At the start, this had a small fan base. Today it has attained cult status. Magnus Walker has specialized in early 911s, including one from each model year in his loft. All of them carry his "signature," which is what he calls his highly detailed unique specimens which often feature references to the 911 R — such as the small round tail lights. One of his best-known signature cars is the silver 1968 model with the decorative blue stripes running lengthwise over the hood and roof, which he himself calls the 68R. Plexiglas side windows with louvers, central tank cap and air vents next to the front lights are included. Walker calls his creations "street-legal racing cars." And indeed, the enthusiastic fan of the 911 has found his way to California's racetracks through the Porsche Club sports scene. The 68R is his first "signature car" to attract the attention of the Porsche community. **Lima Howlett from the band "the Prodigy" persuaded Walker to sell the car built in 2009 for 65,000 US dollars.** That was when the Porsche scene began to take note of Walker. Today the car enthusiast has more than half a million followers on Instagram alone. And somehow they all love this Californian by choice who tends to mumble and who has become a role model for "just doing his thing," for not giving in to convention and for following his gut instincts. **Many dream of doing that but very few people actually dare to live it out.** Clearly, Magnus Walker's cars could be described as four-wheeled dreams.

Silver Metallic

Porsche 911 “68R by Magnus Walker”, 1968/2009
Schuco R Line; Detroit

911 S targa (2.2), 1969
Atlas; Regensburg

Caramel Brown

#Terrorists and the avant-garde

#At the end of the 1960s the 911 was the dream car of the car-manufacturing Germans: its speedometer ranged up to 250 km/h, and the 180-hp 911 S, with its 2.2 liter engine and fuel injection, is in fact capable of reaching 225 km/h. It's definitely capable of occupying the left lane on the highway, where it doesn't really have to fear competitors. **The 911 is the car of choice even for the radical left-wing RAF terrorists and the Baader-Meinhof gang. Andreas Baader liked to use a 911 targa, which he stole from the famous motorsport photographer Rainer Schlegelmilch.** After Baader was arrested and the Porsche seized by the police, Schlegelmilch immediately identified his eggplant-colored 911: The door pocket still contained documents from his trip to the Monaco Grand Prix. The sports cars from Stuttgart are perfectly suited for the long trip — "Grand Turismo" in the truest sense of the word.

The targa, with its sturdy roll bar and large panoramic rear window, fits well visually into the 1970s, where the 1968 protest movement had pushed its way into daily life. The open 911 embodied a certain relaxed attitude that customers appreciated. targa drivers were willing to put up with the necessary fumbling when folding and stowing away the roof section. Wind noise and small leaks also had to be accepted. But all that was nothing compared to the roof constructions of roadsters and convertibles from other manufacturers and model years.

As far as the model mix is concerned, in the 1970s there were two targa models for nearly every three 911 Coupés. Competitors of the 911 S include the eight-cylinder Alfa Romeo Montreal and Lamborghini Urraco, the 6-cylinder mid-engined Italian Maserati Merak and Dino 206, and the 246, respectively, as well as more comfortable models such as the Mercedes-Benz SL and SLC and BMW coupés (3.0 CSL). But none of these vehicles is as versatile as the Porsche — a piece of sporting equipment and everyday car in one. Well, as a targa it is more at home on the highway than the racetrack; its body is noticeably softer than that of the Coupé. But along with the increase in displacement to 2.2 liters achieved starting in September 1969, the torque also increased, and with it, its driving capabilities on country roads and in the city also improved. The straight lines of the 911 had already benefited the year before from extension of the wheelbase by a good five centimeters. Wider tires and rims were also among the driving stabilization measures. **The 1970 model of the 911 S was listed at a price of DM 29,980. A surcharge of 2,220 marks was added for the targa.**

#Can high power ever be wrong?

#Two years after the 2.2-liter engine appeared, Porsche engineers gave the 6-cylinder engine a further displacement boost. **The air-cooled unit now had 2,341 cc displacement and, depending on the model, achieved 130 hp (as a 911 T), 165 hp (911 E) and 190 hp (911 S).** The reason for this precision work on the engine was its adaptation to the emissions legislation in North America, which prescribes operation with regular gasoline. Thanks to the increased combustion chamber volume of its cylinders, the engine of the 911 S now delivered 190 hp despite running on normal gasoline, accelerating the car up to 230 km/h. The improved elasticity and pulling power of the 2.4-liter models were also a plus. As the saying goes: nothing can replace displacement — except more displacement...

But increasing the power as well as reducing compression also had its price. After all, an average of 15 to 20 liters of fuel flowed through the fuel injection system for every 100 kilometers. In response, Porsche also offered an optional tank that had been increased by almost 20 liters to a total of 80 liters. The necessary space was created with a foldable spare wheel. The emergency spare tire can be inflated with the help of a small can of compressed air.

The most distinctive detail of the 2.4-liter 911 S is its front spoiler. This aerodynamic component, which had previously been tested on the racetrack, had a positive effect on directional stability and from that point on was a popular retrofit in the other 911s. Also new was a cast aluminum rim, whose sharp-edged appearance gave it the nickname "meat chopper." In fact, the majority of 911 customers preferred the forged Fuchs aluminum rims.

In the 2.4-liter model, Porsche rearranged the gears of the five-speed transmission. Now the first two gears were on the same level. Also new was the exhaust, now made of stainless steel. This was another form of sustainability. Customers appreciated that they were rustproof and were thus a durable detail.

Bahama Yellow

911 S (2.4), 1971
Jouef; Strasbourg

#A small piece of metal made all the difference: instead of only one small metal lid covering the refueling opening, the 1972 model featured two of them. Number one was traditionally located on the left front fender and can be unlocked using a pull lever located between the door and steering wheel that attached to a short Bowden cable, opening access to the 62-liter fuel tank located above the steering and front axle. Number two was located directly behind the passenger door, at the right rear, where most cars traditionally had the tank opening. And that was the problem. Quite a few gas station attendants — which were still the order of the day in the early 1970s — confused the flap at the rear right of the 911 with the gas tank opening and pumped gasoline in where engine oil was actually supposed to go. **Aficionados of the 911 were already familiar with accessing the oil reservoir from the outside from the 911 R, where a screw cap peeked out from the flank.**

From the start, the weight distribution associated with the rear engine presented chassis developers with challenges that initially lead to additional weights in the bumper ends. Relocation of the dry sump lubrication tank was another measure to shift the weight distribution toward the center of the vehicle. Eleven liters of the lubricating liquid circulate through the air-cooled boxer. And the same flap opening was provided in the body panel in front of the air-cooled boxer to allow the reservoir to be filled with the essential lubricant for operation — at the time the owner's manual called oil consumption of one and a half liters per 1,000 kilometers "normal." Due to the risk of confusion leading to expensive repairs and engine damage, however, these were produced only for the 1972 model year between late summer 1971 and early summer 1972. **Today this unique detail is prized by collectors and allows the 1972 911 to be priced higher than identically equipped 1971 and 1973 models.** Starting in 1973, the big model change with introduction of shock-absorbing safety bumpers was lined up for the 1974 model year. The 911 long remained a "motion detector," as the first Porsche Supercup champion Altfrid Heger called the agile sports car with its unmistakable handling characteristics. But its handling was further refined from generation to generation (and enhanced with safety features such as ABS and the Porsche ESP PSM), so that the 911 was no longer a "fishtailer" to be feared by regular car drivers. Historians are aware, of course, that Porsche was also increasing its displacement from 2.2 to 2.4 liters with this model year.

#The small difference

Tangerine

Porsche 911 S "Oil Flap," 1972
Atlas Collection; Norisring Nuremberg

#The wild '70s

#In gleaming metallic silver or bright signal colors, the 911 targa exuded the zeitgeist of the early 1970s. **As a 911 E, with mid-range but powerful 165 hp from the 2.4-liter engine, it is among the fastest representatives on the still largely congestion-free autobahns.**
It was capable of 220 km/h — the 25 hp more powerful 911 S ran just 10 km/h faster. The 1973 model had a fuel capacity of 85 liters. Its official average consumption was stated as 9.0 liters per 100 km. In actual operation — and with occasional use of the available power — this figure was a mere fantasy. Its acceleration capacity, which catapulted it from a standstill to 100 km/h in 7.9 seconds, was a fact. The S, which at DM 34,700 cost DM 3,700 more, was just 0.9 seconds faster.

While today's professional soccer players mostly show themselves with exotic supercars, the world champions of the day such as Paul Breitner, Berti Vogts and the like, were well outfitted with the 911. The small front spoiler was not the only thing keeping things down to earth. The 911 seemed approachable but still remained a dream for most people. This characteristic remains an integral part of the 911's DNA. And it is one of the magic secrets of its success.

Metallic colors were still among the less frequently chosen options in those years; after all, cars from that era still shared a tendency to form rust. And gleaming metallic surfaces — if the car is to remain attractive in repaired condition — can only be repainted at great expense. Porsche responded with a body made of hot-dip galvanized sheet steel. As a result, the company put an end to rusting through and invented the long-term warranty against rusting through. This once again made Porsche a pioneer, setting an example in terms of sustainability and preparing the ground for the fast-growing popularity of bodywork in glossy metallic paint, for which customers were happy to pay a surcharge.

The front spoiler was also quite fetching. **It is the first aerodynamic component of its kind that came standard with a car. This was quickly imitated, of course.** By both the automotive and the accessories industry. The oil flap at the rear right was already history by the F series in the 1973 model year. But we've already discussed that...

Silver Metallic

Porsche 911 E targa (2.4), 1973
Spark; Berlin

Porsche 911 Carrera RS 2.7, 1972
Welly; Hockenheimring

White/Red

#Porsche was searching for a suitable piece of sports equipment above the 911 S for experienced sport drivers — this group has always been one of Porsche's valued and well served clientele. For use in sports, the Automobile Association requires homologation, i.e. part of specified production quantities. **At the time, the Carrera RS needed production of at least 500 units.** The sales managers took a deep breath. At prices above DM 30,000, this is an ambitious goal. But the distinctive 911 hits like a bomb. Ultimately, 1,308 vehicles will be produced in road trim and another 217 in a stripped-down sports version. **The diet prescribed for the RS is radical: thin glass, no carpet, clock or rear folding seats, and body components made of thin sheet metal and plastic reduced the weight of the lightest Carrera to 900 kilograms.** That's as little as that of a VW Beetle. M 472 is the abbreviation for the more comfortable street version, which can be ordered as an option and into which a number of comfort extras were reintroduced. Their surcharge: DM 2,500 added to the DM 33,000 of the sporty basic model. They all feature front and rear spoilers. The basic color is white. Red, blue and green are available for order, at least as an accent color for the standard Fuchs aluminum wheels and the decorative strip with the Carrera logo on the doors, which is called "Danube waves." Customers who insisted on a different color had to do without the stylish lettering. Metallic colors were frowned upon as "not sporty."

"So, have you now built a sink on top of the back?" was the humorous yet provocative question spontaneously asked by Erich Strenger, a longtime Porsche advertiser, co-founder of *Christophorus* magazine and graphic artist, when he was shown the Carrera RS 2.7 for the first time. The term "ducktail" was then used to refer to the distinctive rear spoiler, which was often retrofitted by other 911 owners. Porsche actually would have liked to eliminate the rear spoiler and instead simply lift the hood a bit when racing — following the example of many owners of Fiat, Abarth and NSU racing cars also equipped with rear engines. But what is aerodynamically and thermally advantageous failed due to the veto of the regulatory authority and ultimately led to the component that developed potentially legendary status in record time. The driving performance is also legendary: With 210 hp, a top speed of 245 km/h and acceleration from 0 to 100 km/h in 5.8 seconds, the Carrera RS 2.7 presented at the Paris Motor Show in October 1972 — shortly before the oil crisis — is Germany's fastest production car. Prior to this, Porsche had a great deal of trouble within its own ranks: Ambitious projects like the prototype racing program, including the outrageously expensive 917, brought the company to the brink of ruin and nearly broke the camel's back. The family was tired of internecine squabbles and prescribed independent management for itself as well as the company. **Head of Development Ferdinand K. Piëch, Production Manager Hans-Peter Porsche and Chief Designer Ferdinand Alexander Porsche have to leave.** F.A. Porsche became independent (with Porsche Design), and its new brand became immortal. After a brief period of independence, Piëch moves further in the direction of Audi and Volkswagen. He would continue to bestow numerous innovations upon the automotive world.

#Ducktails and Danube waves

#One more shovelful

#Motorsport enthusiasts know the endless spiral with which the parameters output, brakes, tires and weight are constantly adjusted to each other and the performance of the vehicle boosted. Just one shovelful more, as they say. But prices also rose along with all that. **In the case of the Carrera RS 2.7, the journey led straight to the Carrera RSR 2.8. The second R reveals the purpose of the street-legal Coupé – racing — and the 2.8 stood for the expanded displacement.** The GT sports car had a rated output of 300 hp and was homologated — meaning it was entitled to race — for Group 4 regulations. The price tag bore the number 59,000. For this amount, the Porsche customer in 1972 could buy two Porsche 911 T models (DM 23,480) and a Mercedes-Benz 200 (DM 13,930) from the Strichacht series.

Forty-nine units of the Carrera RSR 2.8 went into the hands of private individuals like Georg Loos or the Kremer brothers, who competed in the German Racing Championship, Le Mans or the Targa Florio and numerous other races. The more powerful sports car differs visually from the Carrera RS 2.7 due to slightly wider fenders and a front spoiler with installation space for an oil cooler. An even greater success was the Carrera RSR 3.0 model that followed immediately in 1973 with 320 hp, and which maintained the look of the G-series with its wide fenders and a rear wing as became fashionable on the street with the 911 turbo. Just over 100 units of the car were produced. Half of them were driven on streets. The rest on the racetracks of the world. The clientele was more or less the same. And they, including the racing driver, journalist and Jägermeister sponsorship manager Eckhard Schimpf, or the Max Moritz team, were charged a substantial DM 96,000 by Porsche in 1974. Two years later, the turbocharged 934 — a race-ready 930 homologated for Group 4 — cost DM 130,000. **In 1977, Porsche Customer Sports demanded DM 160,000 from its clients for the Group 5 racing variant of the 911, the 935.** This was the story of inflation in the realm of motor sports, which constantly craves improved performance...

White/Red

Porsche 911 Carrera RSR 2.8, 1973
Minichamps; Long Beach

Porsche T8 901-Prototyp, 1962

Porsche 901/911, 1963

Porsche 901, 1964

Porsche 911 (Urmodell), 1965

Porsche 912, 1965

Porsche 911 targa, 1965

Porsche 911 S, 1966

#Generation I (901 and 911)

Porsche 911 R, 1967

Porsche 911 T, 1967

Porsche 911 L, 1968

Porsche 911 "STR 2," 1972

Porsche 911 S targa (2.2), 1969

Porsche 911 S 2.4, 1971

Porsche 911 S "oil flap," 1972

Porsche 911 E targa (2.4), 1972

Porsche 911 Carrera RS 2.7, 1973

Porsche 911 Carrera RSR 2.8, 1973

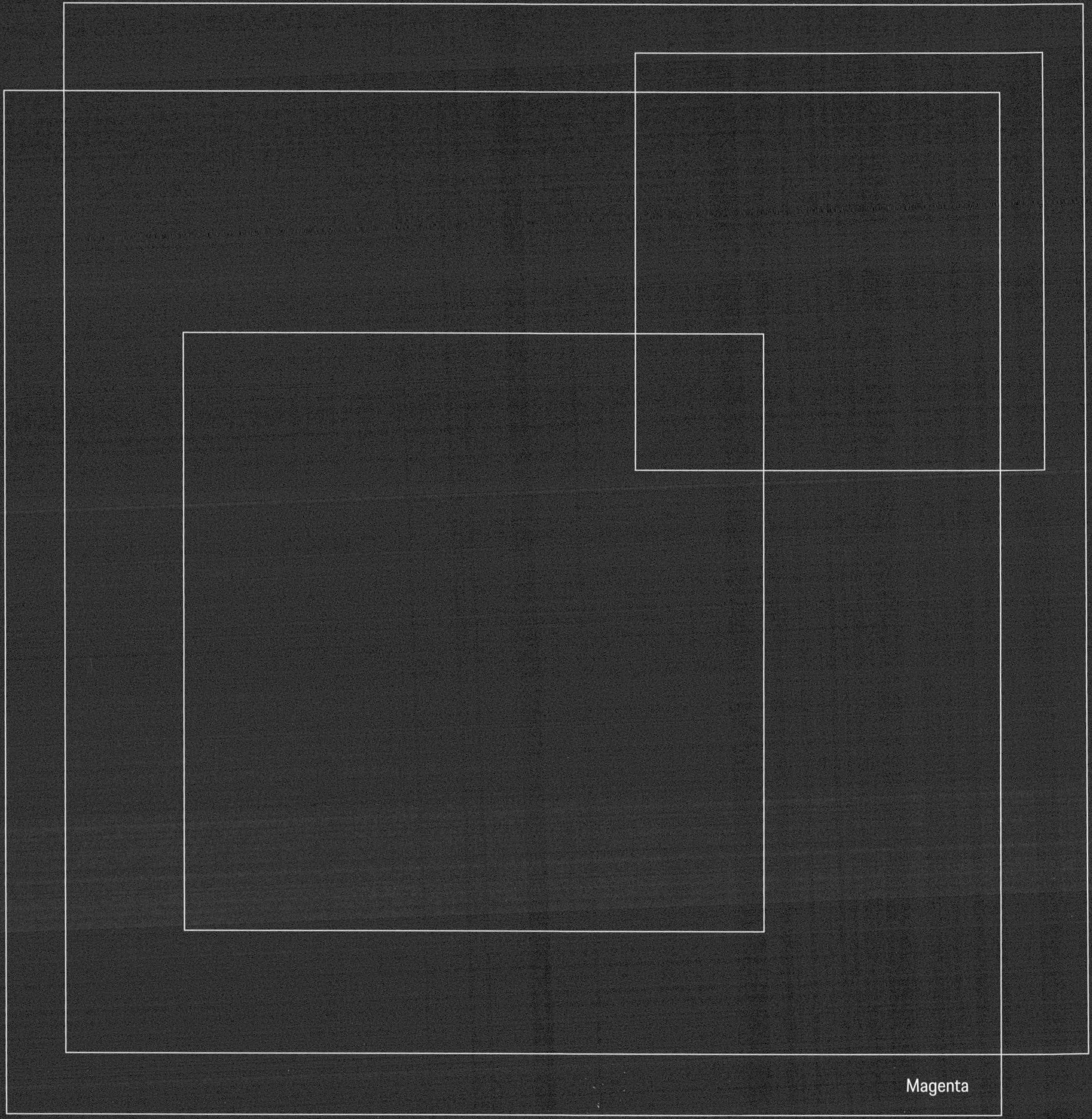

Magenta

#Generation II

(911) and 959

Porsche 911 Carrera 2.7 targa (G model) US export, 1974
Neo; Berlin

Conda Green

#No fear of jostling

#Anatole Lapine was one of the creative young wild ones. Before he joined Porsche, the Riga-born designer had left his mark on Opel. And at Porsche the Latvian began adding things like psychedelic patterns to the range: The eye-catching colors and shapes of the paintwork on the 1970s Martini Porsche originated from his hand. When "Butzi" Porsche clears the field along with the other family members, the baton of the Porsche studio manager was passed to Lapine. And he began with a challenging task: revamping the 911, ten years after its premiere. Once again, motivation for the extensive model update came from the United States, traditionally the brand's most important market. New consumer protection laws demanded damage-free and therefore cost-effective parking collision solutions to comply with the "bumper rules." Car owners were to be protected from damage at speeds of up to five miles per hour. From that point on, the look of most imported vehicles was spoiled with bulky bumpers mounted in front of the body. **With creativity and ingenuity, the Porsche designer turned necessity into a virtue and embellished the 911 with painted, rubber-reinforced aluminum bumpers** that were spring mounted and made visible with characteristic bellows. It all blended harmoniously into the lines of the 911 and remained in this form for a remarkable 16 years of series production. The 911s destined for the US market would also be fitted in Stuttgart with somewhat more voluminous rubber elements on the rear bumper, with red rear turn signals, with turn signal lenses at the front mounted in the bumper and stretching to the side, and with the headlights prescribed for the US along with the accompanying, somewhat bolder headlight ring. A mileage speedometer was likewise mandatory, of course, as were exterior mirrors with warning labels.

Incidentally, in Porsche's own bookkeeping, only the 911s of the 1974 model year were assigned to the G series. Even if one might read differently today in some places and it could be regarded as careless, the H-Series follows in August 1974, after the factory holidays. It continues thus — year after year — with I, K, L and M, before Porsche starts again with A, B, C and D between late summer 1979 — that is, the 1980 model year — and July 1983 (up to the Carrera 3.2). It's complicated and only interesting to hardcore brand and model historians...

From the 1976 model year onwards, Porsche painted the targa bar matte black. This is much cooler and more modern than the shiny stainless steel look. Chrome essentially disappears as a decorative element. Popular instead are eye-catching signal colors like luminous viper green, signal yellow or blood orange. This is also how safety was defined at the time.

It was also Anatole Lapine who was responsible then for the design of the transaxle models 924, 944 and 928. These were not uncontroversial at the time, but the timelessness of their form is all the more impressive today. **By no means does the 928 look as if it has been around more than 40 years.** Neither the car nor its designer could do anything about the insurmountable burden of initially being sold as the successor — and therefore the gravedigger — of the legendary and beloved 911.

As far as the Carrera 2.7 was concerned — without the RS suffix — this 911 was overshadowed by its sister model of the previous generation, which was distinctively designed with the "Danube waves" and ducktail. In terms of engine, the 1974 model is not inferior in any way to the 210 hp 1973 Carrera RS 2.7. Below the 911 Carrera (also with 210 hp) are the 2.7-liter 911 (150 hp) and 911 S (175 hp) models.

Financially speaking, 1974 was a rather bitter year for Porsche; the oil crisis left its mark, there were eight weeks of reduced working hours and at the end of the year, Porsche had not managed to sell 10,000 cars. There were 15,400 911s sold the previous year.

#As is typical for Porsche, the model for the first turbocharged production car was fashioned by the sports car manufacturer itself – in the form of the Carrera RSR turbo, a GT racer designed for the racetrack, which Porsche was racing at the Nürburgring, in Le Mans and on other tracks. A new feature was the impressive "whale fin" of the broad-shouldered racing athlete. Fans reverently called it a monster. Due to the regulations calling for a conversion factor for supercharged engines, the displacement of the supercharged 6-cylinder boxer measures 2.1 liters. But that's enough for 500 hp. **A total of a dozen of these turbo competitors and ideal models for the road vehicle, which celebrated its premiere at the autumn 1974 Paris Salon, were created during the 1974 model year.**
After long trials in racing, turbo technology celebrated its introduction into series production. Wide fenders and the spoiler lip made for a big entrance. The name given was still awkward in the beginning. Porsche tinkered with „Strabo" (for "street turbo") and internally the car runs under the development number 930. In public, the 260 hp bullet is only called "turbo." And the term "turbo" is rapidly becoming a household name, synonymous with speed, superlatives and efficiency. **The timing, on the other hand, was a bit unfortunate, since the energy crisis had previously led to driving bans and a new awareness of the finite nature of global oil reserves.**
The price for the new dream car was DM 65,800 — as much as the cost for eight units of the likewise new VW Golf. A brake system inspired by the 917 racing car came standard, as did electric windows, radio and electric antenna — which was really a big deal at the time! — and the leather upholstery of the avant-garde seating system with integrated headrests. Porsche once again miscalculated when it came to planning quantities: The sales managers also have a maximum of 500 units planned for the turbo, to support the homologation of the visually closely related Carrera RSR 3.0. But with a top speed of over 250 km/h, acceleration from 0 to 100 in six seconds and to 200 in under 20, the car is a dream right from the start. And some were able to fulfill that dream following the start of delivery in March 1975. Between 1975 and 1977, 2,173 units of the 3.0-liter turbo were produced. From August 1975, all Porsche cars were furnished with a body made of hot-dip galvanized steel and were thus protected against rust. The six-year warranty against rusting through remained unique in the automotive world for a very long time. The Porsche top model did as well.

In 2015 a slate gray 911 turbo Carrera (this is now the name of the 930 in the US) was auctioned off for the impressive sum of 1.95 million US dollars. A discreet and unique extra was the switch that could switch off the rear and brake lights in order to outfox any pursuing police cars. **A prominent previous owner of the '76 3.0-liter model auctioned in Monterey, California, was no less than the "King of Cool," Hollywood actor Steve McQueen.** The real film car from the film *Le Mans*, a 1970 911 S, also painted in slate gray, brings a comparatively modest 1,375,000 US dollars four years earlier — also at an auction in Monterey.

#Invited guests

Silver Metallic

Porsche 911 turbo 3.0 (930), 1974
Welly; New York City

#Full-fledged with wings

#After the premiere of the turbo with its distinctive spoilers, the aerodynamic structure of the '73 Carrera RS looked a bit outdated — better suited to its predecessor than to the look of the freshly revamped second generation of the 911. For a time Porsche in Zuffenhausen also used ducktails on the new 911s with their bumper bellows. But customers were eager for the new component, which was also proving to be an enhancement of the rear aerodynamic component in racing. **And Germany's TÜV had safety concerns about the ducktail with respect to protecting pedestrians.**

The rear tail unit celebrated its premiere in 1974 on the 911 Carrera RSR 2.1 turbo, a Group 5 racing car painted in Martini colors, and in a somewhat more subtler form on the Carrera RSR 3.0 and the street-legal turbo. **In 1975, the "safe" rear spoiler in the shape of a fin was part of the surcharge list.**

Fast-driving 911 owners especially prized the optimization of the aerodynamics. And so the aerodynamic enhancements that were standard with the turbo were also used for the 3.0-liter Carrera. Important here was the interaction of the front spoiler lip with the rear spoiler, which was also sometimes derided as a "whale fin." Installing the ducktail increased the top speed by five km/h, as with the predecessor. More important, however, was the significantly improved directional stability and the much more sensitive steering, which benefited from the downforce of the efficient front spoiler, even at fast highway speeds.

For the 1984 model year, with the introduction of the 3.2-liter Carrera, the front and rear spoilers were a fixed part of the list of extras. In turn, the spoiler of the Carrera 3.2 resembles that of the turbo, but in a narrower version without the bulging sides of the 3.3-liter top model.

Even more important than the extra spoiler, enlargement of displacement to three liters and the new, rectangular exterior mirror (electrically adjustable and heated!) for the 1976 model year — the debut of the model year referred to internally as the I Series — is the premiere of the body made from Thyssen steel sheet that was hot-dip galvanized on both sides, accompanied by the long-term warranty against rusting through.

Grand Prix White

Porsche 911 Carrera 3.0, 1976
Kyosho; Herzogenaurach

Porsche 911 Carrera 3.0 (US model), 1976
Neo; Brooklyn/New York City

Silver Green Metalic

#Greetings from America

#Internally, Porsche labels its 1976 911 with the letter J. At the same time, product strategists were reducing the model range somewhat. The Carrera 3.0 model with its 2,994 cc engine, as had already been used in the turbo, now ranked above the 2.7-liter engine in what was now simply called the 911, and below the 3.0-liter turbo — but it featured higher compression and was without turbocharging. **While the turbo unit came with a compression ratio of 6.5:1, the naturally aspirated engines featured a compression ratio of 8.5:1.** For the 2.7, this meant 165 hp, while the 3.0-liter Carrera mobilized a smooth 200 hp. The 930 was known to top that with 60 more. The look of the US version of the 911 differed in part due to its sealed-beam headlamps, which stood a bit more upright and were framed by more abundant headlamp rings. A look at the production figures in those years shows just how important American sales were for Porsche: The 76th model year shows 1,093 Carrera Coupés in "the rest of the world," for example, compared to an impressive 2,079 in the US. **With the Carrera targa, the ratio of 479 to 2,175 was even more pronounced.** And this despite the fact that the 911 with a 2.7-liter engine was withheld from the Americans. In turn, 1,216 units of the 912 E are produced exclusively for the US. And 530 units of the 911 turbo were sent across the big pond, with 644 units going to the rest of the world. Popular extras include the Fuchs rims with stars in the same color as the car, which naturally attracted fans all over the world.

The new safety seats, which dominate the interior in parallel to the debut of the safety bumpers, are mandatory. **The headrests integrated into the backrest become a design feature that furniture designers and interior designers alike were also eager to take up.** From the late '70s on, you could hardly find a dental practice that didn't feature examination chairs resembling the Porsche seats.

#Italian racing nobility

#Conte Ascanio Calvi di Bergolo is one of the aristocratic patrons behind the Piedmont-based Martini liqueurs as well as the company's involvement in professional motorsports. The company, located near Turin, has been known since the middle of the 19th century for its fine herbal liqueurs and vermouth. The former sales representative Alessandro Martini and herbal expert Luigi Rossi gave the company its name, which is still viewed positively today. This is due in part to the company's brilliant history in motorsports, which began in 1969 with financial support of Porsche's activities in the World Sports Car Championship. These days marked the beginning of the colorful age of motorsports. It was not until the end of the 1960s that advertising on sports equipment was permitted. The racing cars of the renowned teams were immediately transformed at international competitions into racing billboards. But it was not until 1971 that Martini, in addition to his brand logo, also developed the red, light blue and dark blue stripes — long characteristic of today's racing cars — and adopted them as a design element. The Italians felt in good hands with Porsche. And the shared successes proved that the members of the factory team operating under the name Martini Porsche were right. Between 1969 and 1977, Martini Porsche celebrated countless victories in sportscar and endurance world championships. **Three joint triumphs at Le Mans represented the absolute high point of the partnership.** And winning the two world championship titles in 1976 — the Sportscar World Championship (with the 935, based on the 911) and the Endurance World Championship (with the 6-cylinder prototype 936) — motivated Porsche to produce special models to celebrate the day. **Both the 924 and the 911 turbo appeared in a "Martini Edition":** White Grand Prix cars with bright red and blue interior elements as well as bodies decorated with the legendary red, light blue and dark blue stripes.

Porsche 911 turbo Martini racing (930), 1976
PremiumX; Copenhagen

#Colorful role model

#It took until 1987 for Porsche to add the 911 turbo into the official delivery program as a Cabriolet and a targa. The reason for this was that, despite the similarities in the way they looked, the body shell of the open variants differed significantly from that of the Coupé on which the turbo was based. A simple swapping out of the various vehicle components was therefore not enough. But customer interest was there and so Porsche set to work at the factory. In the case of a turbo Cabriolet, the sports car manufacturer charges a surcharge of DM 22,000, which in 1989 added up to a total of DM 160,900.

The idea of an open turbo was much older and was realized starting in the mid-'70s by the booming guild of car detailer and tuners. One of them was Rainer Buchmann, who had made a name for himself and his company "bb" with his colorful designs, attractive body modifications and futuristic hi-fi installations. One of his most dazzling creations was the 911 turbo targa with its distinctive rainbow-colored embellishments and royal blue velour interior. It made it onto the cover pages of the car trade media and became a star of the silver screen — ultimately landing a leading role in the gangster comedy "Car-Napping." Meanwhile, the eye-catching soloist got its first role in 1976 at the Photokina, the world's largest photography trade fair, organized in Cologne. And this show business act also provided the reason for the colorful design; it was the corporate colors of the Polaroid company, after all, that put the supercar on the exhibition stand as an eye-catcher.

In fact, to create the car, Buchmann needed a 911 targa as a base and a 911 turbo to supply parts. This ultimately made the vehicle even more expensive than the surcharge charged by Porsche a good ten years later. Buchmann welded another 40 kg of sheet steel into the targa body at the time and gave it the stiffness of the Coupé.

Rainer Buchmann is said to have sold the used car in 1982 for DM 80,000 — a brand-new 3.3.0-liter turbo cost just DM 12,000 more than that.

Porsche 911 turbo targa bb "Rainbow," 1976
Neo; Zurich

Porsche 911 targa, 1976
Minichamps; Ludwigsburg

Silver Metallic

#Safety and family spirit

#"The threshold to success measures just 27 centimeters," stated the headline of a Porsche advertisement showing a short-legged Bassett hound climbing into the passenger footwell of a 911 targa. In the years long before the SUV boom and the ubiquitous electronic assistants and control systems, flat vehicles with a low center of gravity were considered safe cars with good road holding. A clear point for Porsche. Even though the performance of sports cars — especially in the absence of electronic safety systems — placed special demands on the driving qualities and sense of responsibility of their drivers. In the view of the marketing managers in Stuttgart and Ludwigsburg (the headquarters of German sales), this in turn unites Porsche drivers and gives them a special feeling of being a family. The company's advertisements say: **"The Porsche family has what many families lack — the feeling of "us": the same interests, shared goals, time for each other.** And time for the hobby of driving a car that we all love, driving better than others — and fairer too. In an exceptionally safe, exceptionally reliable and exceptionally attractive automobile."

Porsche also advertised the 911 as a family car at that time; after all, 67 percent of all 911 drivers were female drivers. These were often wives who also appreciated the easily accessible luggage space behind the seats. "To be sure: the Porsche is still not a family sedan. Rather, it is a good example of how family and a sports car can be combined well." Advertising poetry of the late '70s...

And the company was successful: The 250,000th Porsche, a 911 Coupé, rolled off the assembly line on June 3, 1977. The stars on the five-spoked Fuchs rim were often still polished in those days and thus visually prominent. That vanished in favor of fashionable black — and also made production cheaper. Porsche has also eliminated the chrome ring hidden under the painted headlight ring — an improvement and cost-cutting measure suggested by a Porsche employee who was rewarded with an attractive bonus for this idea. This kind of idea management, as such programs for improvements suggested by employees are often called, is standard in almost all companies today.

#The finalist that wasn't

#Porsche fans were already familiar with the SC abbreviation from the 356. It adorns the final model in the 4-cylinder series. At the end of the '70s, quite a few people suspect that the final round for the 911 had begun. After all, the eight-cylinder 928 was the designated successor in the showroom. Porsche CEO Ernst Fuhrmann acknowledged in an interview: **"It will be another two to three years before the 911 can be discontinued."** But Porsche had not adequately considered their enthusiastic as well as loyal clientele, which continued to drive the 911. And the decision was made easy for them: The 911 SC was fully mature, with an 180 hp 3.0-liter engine and an attractive price: While the Carrera 3.0 still cost DM 47,700, the SC was available for a mere 39,900. The model, which was initially situated between the 911 S and 911 Carrera, could be recognized by the slightly wider rear fenders, among other things.

The body of the 911 had been made of hot-dip galvanized sheet steel since 1976, giving the car a six-year warranty against rusting through — a sensation at a time when early death by rust was the primary cause of the last trip to the junkyard. A further admired detail were the inner door locks, which were now mounted in the form of rotary knobs. This was the end of the game for thieves, whose manual skills involved abruptly opening cars with a simple wire inserted through the door seals. Manual was also the magic word for most Porsche drivers: the three-speed Sportomatic, which was still available by special request and for a surcharge of DM 1,200, led a marginal existence. But Porsche didn't remove them from the range until 1979. The 911 SC comes standard with a five-speed manual transmission. Porsche offers a total of six different engine configurations for the 911 SC for various markets and climate zones. All have secondary air injection. **A catalytic converter is mandatory for those sold to Japan and the US.** In Germany, the catalytic converter is first introduced in the mid-'80s with the then up-to-date 911 Carrera 3.2 — the engine output drops from 231 to 217 hp due to the accompanying engine adjustments. Prior to the release of the Carrera 3.2, which initially had 231 hp, the performance of the 911 SC was boosted to 188 hp at its start (1979) and to 204 hp in 1981. Among other things, the compression of the boxer engine was increased for this purpose. Now the use of higher octane super gasoline is necessary again.

As a further advertising measure in 1977, Porsche sent two 911 SC to the Safari Rally in Kenya. That had been raised 28 centimeters, featured a reinforced chassis and ram protection, and had been strengthened to 250 hp. On the tortuous route they battled to a respectable second-place finish.

Silver Metallic

Porsche 911 SC, 1977
Minichamps; Herzogenaurach

Porsche 911 turbo 3.3 (930), 1977
Minichamps; New York City

Guards Red

#Evergreen

#Three years and 2,173 units later, the 911 turbo received a comprehensive update for the 1978 model year. The focus was on increasing the combustion chamber volume from three to 3.3 liters. This also increased the engine output from 260 to 300 hp. The look remained unchanged, essentially unchanged, because the 3.3-liter models could be identified by the slightly enlarged rear spoiler with circumferential rubber lip. **The more voluminous spoiler now also accommodated the intercooler mounted above the 6-cylinder boxer.**

In this form, the model proved to be a true evergreen, because while the sister model with its narrower naturally aspirated engine was still experiencing various capacity enlargements, the 3.3-liter turbo — aside from various smaller model update measures, such as the introduction of a five-speed transmission (1989), for example — remained unchanged in the delivery program until the appearance of the 3.3-liter turbo in the same look as the model-maintained 964 in 1989. The list price for the top model in June 1977 was DM 78,500. Twelve years later, in April 1989, the price list shows it at DM 138,800. The leather upholstery is included here — and yet there are a few customers who prefer the more non-slip fabric upholstery. A metallic paint finish is also included in the standard delivery and any desired color can be realized for a reduced surcharge of DM 1,060 (compared to DM 2,350 for all other models, in 1984). The new, powerful brake system with four-piston fixed calipers and internally ventilated, perforated discs, like the one that caused a furor in the Le Mans racer 917 is also standard — in addition to minor details such as the passenger exterior mirror, a high-pressure headlight cleaning system and fog lamps. Characteristic for the turbo are the Fuchs forged aluminum rims in 16-inch format.

Incidentally, Porsche offers just three 911 variants in the 1978 model year, with the 911 SC Coupé, SC targa and turbo 3.3. **In 2018, thanks to a much larger range of products, those interested in 911 are spoiled for choice with no fewer than 23 different model** variants to choose from, all of which can be further individualized according to their wishes and financial possibilities.

One of the outstanding features of the 3.3-liter turbo is its unique combination of drive comfort and exceptional performance, which culminates in a top speed of 260 km/h. This enables long drives with high average speeds. This is unique in the automotive world of the '70s. And it will set the style for the 911 turbo of every generation.

Porsche 911 Carrera 3.2; 1983
Kyosho; Porsche Zentrum Nuremberg

Guards Red

#Under the skin

#Just in time for the 20th birthday of the 911, early enough for the model year 1984, the black lettering on the rear fog lights now integrated into the rear light band is replaced by the lettering. At first glance, this is the only modification of the type to the look that has become highly familiar for a decade now. But far more important is what happens under the body. There it worked with a 6-cylinder engine with a displacement of 3.2 liters and 231 hp.

The golden rule at Porsche has always been that performance can only be increased if consumption can be reduced at the same time. No sooner said than done: In the 911 Carrera a new electronic engine control system including thrust cut-off and increased compression were responsible for this. Porsche engineers were devoting further attention to the chain tensioner, which has so far proven to be the Achilles' heel of the engine. From now on it works hydraulically and maintenance-free. Modified heat exchangers benefit the heating performance and thus all occupants. Consumption and driver benefit from the newly developed five-speed transmission with the designation G50. But not before the 1987 model year. Prior to this, the slightly modified predecessor generation had to cope with the increase in power — the 911 turbo's transmission, which was designed for higher power and torque, only had four gear steps. The capacity expansion would benefit not only European Porsche drivers but also customers in the North American and Japanese markets, for which the engines are designed for operation on unleaded fuel. After all, the exhaust gases have for years been cleaned there by catalytic converters. This only became an issue in Europe in the mid-1980s. **For the German Carrera 3.2 customer, this meant giving up 14 hp from model year 1987 onwards.**

There was a plus in terms of weight, as a well-equipped Carrera 3.2 weighs in at 1,280 kilos. The 911 originally weighed just under 1,100 kg, and even a 74 model was just 20 kg heavier than its ancestor. The added weight is due to the newly designed technical components of the more powerful car, but convenient extras and increased demands for environmental friendliness also have an impact here. **All in all, the Carrera 3.2 is considered the "roundest" of all the original 911s.**

Porsche 911 Carrera Cabriolet, 1983
Minichamps, Pfalzpaint

Continental Orange

#At the beginning of the 1980s, the convertible automobile was threatened with extinction. With the demise of the British automotive industry, the original roadsters were also laid to rest. Only vehicles like the Alfa Romeo Spider, Mercedes-Benz SL (W 109), Morgan +8, Rolls-Royce Corniche Convertible and VW Golf Cabriolet remain true to the open-top design. US consumer protection advocate Ralph Nader nearly spelled the end for the convertible. He became known for a study published under the name "Unsafe at any Speed." The background for the harsh criticism in a time of explosive growth in the use of automobiles was primarily the lack of safety. Porsche responded, for example, with the 911 targa in the form of a "safety convertible," the successor to the 356 Cabriolet.

At the beginning of the '80s, however, the open-top car celebrated its renaissance. And as in the 1950s, the initiative was once again based on the high-volume US market. The Porsche boss at the time, Peter Schutz, strengthened the 911, which had been down for the count in Zuffenhausen, and sparked new impetus with the cabriolet concept car presented at the IAA in 1981 — 16 years after the last convertible 356. **The project ran in Zuffenhausen and Weissach under the name "Roadster."** The starting shot was fired in February 1981. The ideas had already become reality the following year: The first completely open 911 appeared at the Geneva Salon in the spring of 1982. As a slender SC, in Pure White. It was an instant crowd favorite. Porsche listed it at DM 64,500. But the hefty price (the added price compared to the Coupé is almost DM 9,000) does not dampen demand. The first annual production lot had already been sold before the trade show had ended. SC stands for "Super Carrera" and in '82 it meant three liters of displacement and 204 hp, at the end of 1983 it became the Carrera with 3.2 liters capacity and 231 hp. Available as Coupé, targa and Cabriolet. And from then on, the Cabriolet remains a firmly established part of the 911 range.

#Open to the elements

An advantage for Porsche in the development of the convertible was that the design changes for the transformation from targa to Cabriolet remain manageable. Thus, a small team of five engineers succeeded in realizing a series-produced concept within two months. They were able to crack the toughest nut with the development of the stable, lined, self-tensioning hood with a plastic rear window that could be opened. The elimination of the roll bar and panoramic rear window reduced the weight of the car by 15 kilos. **For long winters — for the bold surcharge of DM 10,000 — there is a hand-made hardtop that looks, when assembled, like it has been cut out of the Coupé's face.** In 1985 Porsche demanded almost DM 4,000 for the optional electric operation of the convertible top. In Stuttgart they promptly named it the "Hollywood version."

Cabriolet, by the way, comes from the French and means "leap into the air." In view of the driving pleasure that every Porsche offers, all Porsches should actually be called Cabriolets...

Since 1981, by the way, only hot-dip galvanized steel sheet has been used. Self-confidently, and acknowledged by the public with appreciative admiration, Porsche extends the warranty against rusting through to seven years.

#On any terrain

#The four-wheel-drive Cabriolet concept car shown at the IAA 1981 followed the homework of the developers from Weissach. **It ultimately led to the 959 supercar, the fastest production car in the world at the time, and to the introduction of all-wheel drive into the 911 product range.** Development efforts under competitive pressure — the constant motivation of all outstanding motorsports activities — marks an important stage in the growth of these development managers. The 911 derivatives internally numbered 953 and 954 were interim reports on this activity. The 911 SC RS 4x4 was designated 953, a four-wheel-drive 911 that passed its performance test with flying colors by winning the legendary Dakar Rally. In autumn 1983, a total of three vehicles were built for the '84 edition of the approximately three-week and 14,000 km long off-road rally across North and Central Africa. This was preceded by development runs with a prototype, which the development team built quickly on the basis of the former company car of their boss, a red Carrera 3.2 — naturally with a slender body. In

order to reliably convert the sometimes lower-quality North African fuels into energy, the compression ratio and power output of the engine were reduced. In rally trim, the 231 hp boxer now mobilizes 225 hp. Digital engine electronics were also being used for the first time in this demanding competitive environment. In contrast to the later 959, the power distribution was still rigid with 31 percent on the front axle and, correspondingly, 69 percent at the rear. And for the misleading, since, Porsche engineers raised the ground clearance from the standard 120 millimeters to a high 27 centimeters; use of a reinforced chassis was included. A 260-liter tank is also part of the scope of modifications.

Even before the 953, Porsche created the 954, better known as the 911 SC RS. But with a series limited to just 20 vehicles, the 911 SC RS is also more of a matter for die-hard 911 and Porsche experts. It comes in Pure White, with a turbo widebody, slimmed down to the bare essentials. **Its weight is reduced to just over 1,000 kilograms — compared to the 911 turbo, which is almost confusingly similar in appearance, this is a considerable reduction of over 250 kilograms.** Even the steel sheets are rolled thinner for this purpose. Aluminum hoods were no longer up for discussion; they were taken as a given, as was a thin glass front window and the use of plastics wherever stability allowed. The light skin concealed the 255 hp 3.0-liter engine taken from the 911 SC and further developed. In competition trim, 280 hp was available. These vehicles, homologated in accordance with the new Group B regulations that came into force in 1982, found their way into rally racing and into collectors' hands. The public gazed at the concept car named Group B with which Porsche unveiled the 959 — likewise produced in accordance with Group B specifications — at the IAA 1983...

Kiln Red Metallic

Porsche 911 Carrera 4x4 (953), 1983
Spark; Deauville

#With the 1982 motorsport season, the World Automobile Association FIA (or its FISA sports department, which existed in this form until 1993) redefined the world of motorsport. From then on, instead of the group classification of one to six that applied for series and prototype vehicles, the numbers A, B and C would apply. For example, touring cars, of which at least 5,000 vehicles were produced in series within a year, fell under Group A homologation. **Group B, on the other hand, required only 400 vehicles, while sport approval of an evolution of that type required 20.** And in the Group C category, the sports car prototypes of a Porsche 956 or 962 could be found. While Group A sports cars initially caused a sensation, especially in the newly booming touring car series — such as in France and the DTM — in rallying, Group B was becoming immortal — although use of this word is misleading, since the increasingly extreme Group B rally monsters were catapulting both their drivers and the sport into the abyss. After a series of serious accidents, the decision to end Group B in rallying was made in the mid-1980s. Instead, use of vehicles homologated in accordance with Group A regulations was also prescribed there from 1986 onwards. That was still in the future when the Group B concept car based on the 911 turbo debuted at a motor show in 1983. At that time, a circuit racing career for Group B cars was still conceivable, since Ferrari was also developing a comparable vehicle with the 288 GTO.

Internally, the project was originally called 911 Group B. However, at the time of the definition of the specifications, the numbers 959 (for the road and rally version) and 961 (for the circuit version) were also defined. Even before Porsche chose the 911 for the Group B project, the 924 or 944 were still under discussion. After all, the Stuttgart-based company was also involved in motorsport with its high-volume models at the beginning of the 1980s. **However, the technicians relied on four-wheel drive for their Group B sports car right from the start.** And this was difficult to achieve with the front-engine transaxle models. The traditional rear engine had the clear advantage.

The center of attention exhibited in Frankfurt in September still came with a smooth body without any additional openings. These would be modeled into the plastic body in the course of developing the (small) production vehicle that was to be built later.

#Exhibition soloist

White Pearl

Porsche Gruppe B Concept; 1983
Spark; Stuttgart-Zuffenhausen

#The scale on the speedometer ranged up to 340 km/h. According to the factory that was an actual 315, or precisely 317 (according to AMS measurement). During a supercar comparison test in 1989, the trade magazine *auto, motor und sport* measured an additional model — one that had been discreetly boosted in performance at the factory (officially, the somewhat "hotter" 959 as an S, as in sport) — at an impressive 339 km/h. Thus, in the mid-'80s, the 959 attained a place on the automotive Mount Olympus as one of the fastest street-legal production vehicles of all time. It was bettered only by the Ruf CTR, which was aerodynamically superior due to its slender lines and was also based on the 911. The crankshaft of the ams test car produced 515 hp, although the registration papers normally stated 450. Responsible for the power output was a 2.85-liter boxer with air-cooled cylinders and water-cooled four-valve heads — as had previously been used with success on the 935 and 956 C — which was impressively and forcefully supercharged and forcefully by twin turbochargers. **A new feature was their sequential arrangement, which provided smooth power even at low engine speeds which certainly did not diminish at the top.** Traction was provided by a variably controllable all-wheel drive with adjustable torque distribution and adjustable limited slip differentials. The tires thus gripped the asphalt in such a way that it took only 3.7 seconds to sprint to 100 km/h. The gears were shifted by means of a 6-speed transmission. **Officially, however, it was a five-speed transmission with an additional off-road gear, because otherwise the car would not have been able to meet the registration requirements;** in off-road gear — actually the first — the measured outside noise was too loud. But in what was officially first gear — and in reality, second — it worked.

Other high-tech features of this superlative car of those years included a chassis with adjustable ride height and suspension with selectable shock-absorber control, automatic air pressure control in the magnesium wheels with hollow spokes, ABS and power steering. The body was another innovation: It consisted of high-tech fiberglass and was placed over the steel skeleton, which otherwise would support the sheet steel body of the 911. Added to this were the doors and trunk lid made of aluminum. Although the two filling openings in the body of the 1972 911 caused confusion, the aerodynamically shaped shell of the 959 had three: The fuel tank opening was moved from the left front fender into the trunk lid. The flap for refilling the engine oil was now again placed on the right, behind the passenger door. And mirroring that opening, the 959 had an opening for refilling the hydraulic oil at the left rear. Experts celebrated Porsche for the appearance of the DM 420,000 supercar. Engineers working with Helmuth Bott, head of development, had reported that between the IAA presentation of the Group B and the start of testing in 1984, they were forced to decide not to introduce some of their high-tech ideas into the car because they otherwise would simply never have been able to finish it. And the costs would certainly have been even further out of control. **Instead of the originally estimated DM 300,000, the showpiece actually cost an additional DM 120,000.** Critics called the total 292 units — 29 of which were in the aforementioned sport version — "the company's most expensive promotional gift." When Porsche was in crisis in the early 1990s, then-CEO Wendelin Wiedeking pointed to the supercar produced in 1986 and 1987 as a symbol of the company's mistakes: Technology-loving, complex constructions, a lack of synergies with other models and outdated production methods. Yet the Porsche 959 was and remains an icon of the brand as well as a trailblazer for technologies that soon were introduced in high-volume series production and thus became affordable. The path for technical innovations always runs from the top down.

#Automotive feasibility study

Silver Metallic

Porsche 959, 1985
Atlas Collection; Hockenheimring

#In a rush

#The 1970s and '80s were a time of great change for car tuners. As such, garages could make a name for themselves if they understood how to produce their own interpretations while adding increased performance, comfort, equipment or extravagance to standard vehicle models. The Opel Manta, VW Golf GTI, BMW 3 Series, Mercedes-Benz 190 E as well as the Porsche 911 were some of the most popular tuned car models in those days. Most tuning on a Porsche was focused on modifying the exterior and interior. The Allgäu-based workshop of long-time Porsche and VW dealer Alois Ruf was undoubtedly among the more "hands-on" of these. And for him, the focus of interest was on driving performance and performance.

Porsche tuner Alois Ruf offered a 911 turbo with expanded 3.3-liter displacement even before the factory did. Ruf registered himself as an automobile manufacturer in 1981. And he made his Allgäu-based company world-famous with his bright yellow CTR, presented in 1987. The color gave the car the nickname "Yellowbird," which is still used today in many computer games. The 469 hp 6-cylinder engine, its combustion chamber volume slightly enlarged to 3.4 liters and with boost pressure of 1.1 bar, accelerates the Ruf CTR to a phenomenal 342 km/h. This makes it even faster than the 959. A world record. In its day, and for a long time to come.

The fact that the yellow rocket effortlessly reached speeds well beyond the 300 km/h mark was the result of extensive effort. That included the cylinder bore being made one millimeter larger, forged pistons, specially manufactured camshafts, work on the (cylinder) head, modified charge air cooling and Motronic. First and foremost, the slender Carrera body helped minimize drag, in line with a customized front apron and narrow rear wing. The rear seats were also removed, as were the insulation material and underbody protection. A welded roll cage was added as a reinforcing safety measure. In the end, the scale stopped at 1,150 kilograms. That was just less under 200 kg lighter than its sibling 300 hp production model, the 911 turbo 3.3. There were also firmer shock absorbers, and the height was lowered by 40 millimeters. **The car sprints from a standstill to 100 km/h in 4.2 seconds, and to 200 km/h in 10.5** — as the former racing driver and automotive journalist Paul Frère could attest.

The straight-line stability as well as the modified brake system (with Brembo calipers and discs from the 962 C) earned praise from *auto, motor und sport* and "sport auto" editor Norbert Haug. Ruf launched a small series of 20 vehicles in 1988. Unit price: DM 300,000.

Yellow

Ruf CTR "Yellowbird," 1987
Spark; Paris

Porsche 911 turbo 3.3 Cabriolet "Slant Nose" (exclusively Porsche), 1987
Altaya; Los Angeles

Lemon Yellow

#Flat speedster

#The Italians were setting the fashion once again; the flat flounders from Maserati, Ferrari, Lamborghini and Co. were shaping the tastes for contemporary sports car fashion at the time.
The characteristic appearance of the 911, with the fenders loved by Ferry Porsche and which acted as sight lines, looked a bit "old-fashioned." Today, the classic 911 lines have long since developed into a stylish evergreen. In the 1970s and '80s it looked like a reference to the style of its own brand.

On the racetrack, the traditional terrain of true sports cars, the fenders of the 911 were streamlined with the appearance of the 935. In 1976, the characteristic 911 fenders vanished and were replaced with flat fenders in order to achieve the lowest possible aerodynamic drag. **So it was only natural that some 911 buyers wanted this sporty look for the road as well.** Until the 1984 model year, Porsche left fulfillment of these wishes to tuners and finishers, who offered a range of various slant nose constructions for sale. None of them, however, in the customary Porsche quality. This changed with the slant nose offered ex works starting in 1983 as part of the Special Request Program. This program developed into the Porsche Exclusive Program, which has now been established for a long time and the scope of which can hardly be exaggerated. In the spring of '84, the brochure for the Special Request range had just twelve pages, including components for the 944 Transaxle sports car. **In addition to the slant nose fenders with integrated folding headlights, air intake openings were also offered in the rear fenders — also inspired by racing.** Added to this was leather work, center consoles with a telephone and hi-fi systems. Another technical highlight was the handwheel in the center console for adjusting the boost pressure — this "steam wheel" was also familiar to motorsport enthusiasts.

#Shortened rear cover

#At the IAA in 1987, Porsche presented a special kind of eye-catcher to the public: the 911 Cabriolet, equipped with a flatter windscreen and a rear cover that transformed the 2+2 into a pure two-seater. **The name of the new 911 was new and yet still familiar: Speedster.** Unlike the all-weather, lined convertible top, the Speedster hood was only intended as makeshift protection from the elements. Another special feature of the exhibition model: The windscreen and interior cover were removable to make room for a large plastic cover that reduced the front area of the vehicle and improved its aerodynamics. In this variant, known as Clubsport, the Speedster quickly became a monoposto. **This version, however, remained an exotic caprice, but the Speedster was immediately popular. The 356 Speedster, conceived at the time as a low-cost, streamlined entry-level model, has since become the most coveted of all 4-cylinder boxer models among Porsche enthusiasts and classic car collectors.** The new model, which went into series production for the 1989 model year — at a time when special automobiles were pushing into previously unfamiliar price regions — spontaneously met with great enthusiasm. The 911 Speedster was available both with the originally shown narrow body as well as with flared fenders in the turbo look. **2,100 copies were produced in parallel with the start of the 964 generation.** It was followed in 1993 by 930 units of the narrow 911 Speedster of the 964 generation — again at the end of model series production, in parallel to the premiere of the 993 generation — plus 15 wide Speedsters with fenders in the turbo look. After another break, Porsche produced another 356 units of the 997 generation 911 Speedster in 2010 to mark the 25th anniversary of Porsche Exclusive Manufaktur. And on June 8, 2018, on the 70th anniversary of the company, Porsche will present itself with a one-of-a-kind anniversary model based on the 991 generation, which ends in 2019. It clears the path for low-volume series production of 1,948 units of the 991 Speedster — likewise part of the reminiscence that is "70 years of Porsche sports cars."

Guards Red

Porsche 911 Speedster Clubsport, 1987 (911 Speedster, 1989)
Schuco; Norisring Nürnberg

Porsche 911 Carrera 3.2 Factory Turbo Look, 1989
Minichamps; Manhattan

Guards Red

#When dreams come true

#Even the characteristic sound with which the door of the 911 closes. Without clanking or a loud noise — just mechanically clean and honest. A bright "plop." A sound that can be distinguished from hundreds of other doors. Put the key into the ignition on the left, turn it briefly and the 6 cylinders join the tune. Its sound is sonorous, rich and powerful. The fan wheel sings along. Double clutching with the five-speed transmission is a pleasure. After a brief bit of practice, the dance on the standing pedals is rewarded with harmonious sounds made by shifting gears and accelerating. The seat position is comfortable even for someone who is tall. The windshield seems huge but in fact the driver is sitting very close to it. The standard steering wheel is a little on the large side but it helps limit the effort required to steer, since the 964 generation 911 does without servo support. In combination with the ample tires, this means there is no reason to hold back. When parking, but also on the track. Long drawn-out highway curves, negotiated at high speeds, build up the forearm muscles. A grandiose power play with the powerful machine. The 3.2-liter boxer in the rear of the 911 turbo — which looked just like the 3.3-liter 911 turbo and whose equipment variant is illogically called "factory turbo look" (Werksturbolook, or WTL for short) — produced 231 hp. This became part of the optional delivery program in the '80s — in 1984 Porsche listed the 911 Carrera Coupé at DM 61,950. **The option with the number 491, for "turbo look, but Coupé," cost another DM 24,900.**

The top speed suffered a little from the larger front surface of the wide 911. The handling, on the other hand, benefited from the wide track and more powerful brake system behind the Fuchs rims in 16-inch format. The optional differential lock (DM 1,220 for all models in the Porsche range, even the 911 turbo) also ensured proper power transmission. The 911 can also move sideways, if desired. **Caution is always required on tram tracks, in wet conditions and on changing road surfaces within and outside the city limits. Vehicle control is preferred.** Driving skills help when guiding ABS-free cars safely through their lifetimes. The sound of the 6-cylinder engine is marvelous, especially beyond 4,000 rpm. Like a choir of trumpets, the engine tunes into the concert of power and performance. The unfiltered way in which the occupants perceive the vehicle and its movement in time and space harmonizes well with this.

Porsche 911 Carrera 3.0, 1976

Porsche 911 turbo 3.0 (930), 1974

Porsche 911 Carrera 3.0; 1975

Porsche 911 turbo
"von Karajan" (980), 1975

Porsche 911 targa, 1976

Porsche 911 turbo targa bb, 1976

Porsche 911 SC, 1977

Porsche 911 Speedster Clubsport, 1987

Porsche 911 Carrera (3.2), 1983

#Generation II (911) and 959

Porsche 911 Carrera Cabriolet, 1983

Porsche 911 Carrera 4x4 (953), 1983

Porsche Gruppe B Concept, 1983

Porsche 959, 1985

Ruf CTR "Yellow Bird," 1987

Porsche 911 turbo Cabriolet, 1987

Porsche 911 Speedster Clubsport, 1987

Porsche 911 Carrera Werksturbolook, 1989

Turquoise Metallic

#Generation III

(964) and Panamericana

Porsche 911 Carrera 4 (964), 1988
Atlas Collection; Hamburg-Blankenese

Guards Red

#On all fours

#After the premiere of the all-wheel drive Cabriolet concept car at the IAA '81, the development work and production of the over Über-911 — the 959 — and the victories at the legendary Paris-Dakar Rally, Porsche brought the all-wheel drive into series production. **The third generation of 911 was released just in time for the 25th anniversary of the model,** as the Carrera 4 with all-wheel drive. The next year, Porsche followed up with the rear-drive Carrera 2. Also available on request with the new Tiptronic switch, which can be operated manually or automatically as required. With the generation operating internally under Code 964, the displacement and power output increased to 3.6 liters and 250 catalyst-cleaned hp, with double ignition and knock control included. The metal exhaust catalytic converter had been tested previously in racing, responded faster than its ceramic predecessor and did not cut engine performance to the extent previously experienced. Customers were paying even more attention to the modern blessings for comfort and safety that had been withheld from the 911 until that point: power steering and ABS. The front torsion bars previously used in the 356 and 911 were discarded and replaced with more modern MacPherson struts, light alloy wishbones and coil springs. The Fuchs rims were also passé. For the time being, they were replaced with disc wheels reminiscent of manhole covers. **The 964s were visually recognizable by their more voluminous bumpers as well as the dark red through-dyed, slightly inclined rear light band and the hood with the new, electrically extending rear wing.** The many new technical parts and the aerodynamically clad underbody were not visible from the outside. Airbags for drivers and passengers would also be standard from 1990 on. The Porsche CEO Heinz Branitzki (1988-1990) saw the best and most mature of all 911s to date as "the 911 for the next 25 years." He was thoroughly mistaken in that, as the next, fourth generation of 911, the 993, was already in the starting blocks in autumn 1993. The company was experiencing challenging economic times. The 911 was expensive. Not only for the customer, but also for the company. **The production of the 964, which has been further developed from the original 911, was complex and therefore costly.** The production of one car required 95 hours — two years later Porsche was able to increase the pace and reduce production time to 76 hours. In those days, Porsche was a perennial takeover candidate and was happy to get external orders such as the contract production of the Mercedes-Benz 500 E.

For its anniversary, in-house test and development drivers staged a ballet on the site of the test track in Weissach with 200 Indian red Carrera 4s, which went to US dealers.

#Open at the top

#The sudden success of the open-top 911 leaves no doubt regarding the Cabriolet concept. The Cabriolet was a part of the new generation of the 911 from the start. And so it remained for the time being with the triad of Coupé, targa and Cabriolet, familiar since 1982. In 1989, the rear-wheel drive Carrera 2 followed its all-wheel drive sibling, which had been in production for a year. It also had the new rear wing, which automatically extended at 80 km/h. **The spoiler can also be put up with the push of a button. Critics call the button something for "posers."** Officially, the mechanism makes it easier to clean that body part.

In 1990, Porsche introduced the Tiptronic, a four-stage automatic transmission. The marketing language refers to a "intelligent, powershift drive system." Porsche charges a DM 6,500 surcharge for this. New colors, such as star ruby, speed yellow or Wimbledon green metallic bring candy-colored variety into play. In addition to the classic colors like Grand Prix White and Indian red, the color palette offers a range of metallic colors for the surcharge of DM 1,780. **For the more distinctive special colors, the company charges DM 2,335.** And for 911 customers for whom the choice of colors was not sufficient, Porsche offered the option — for a DM 3,480 surcharge — to have the new car painted in any color imaginable. Another rarely ordered extra was the DM 1,875 tarpaulin, which could be used as a weatherproof way to seal up the car even when the top was open.

Incidentally, with the introduction of the 964 generation, the "classic" 911 would initially continue to be produced in parallel. The production of the Carrera 3.2 and turbo only ended well into 1989.

Wimbledon Green Metallic

Porsche 911 Carrera 2 Cabriolet (964), 1989
Minichamps; Herzogenaurach

Porsche Panamericana, 1989
Neo; Herzogenaurach

Dragonfly Turquoise Metallic

#During the eight generations of the 911 to date, there have been four designers who have left their mark on the model: First and foremost was Ferdinand Alexander Porsche, nicknamed "Butzi," who laid the foundation stone for the iconic car. He was followed by the Latvian Anatole Lapine, whose work kept the 911 up-to-date for a long time. He succeeded in making US bumpers attractive worldwide, establishing matte black accents and lending wings to the 911. **Since 2004, Michael Mauer has been responsible for Porsche's design language, including the 911.** And in between, from 1989 to 2004, it was the Dutchman Harm Lagaaij (or Lagaay, depending on the spelling) who got Porsche in top shape. Before Lagaaij became Porsche's head of design, he made a name for himself with the experimental and exceptional BMW Roadster Z1. His work at Porsche began before his detour to BMW, because Lagaaij had already worked on Anatole Lapine's team between 1971 and 1977. His premiere piece as chief designer was a topic of discussion at the '89 IAA. With the bright turquoise Panamericana concept car, the successor to Anatole Lapine outlined what the future could look like for Porsche. Indeed, the extreme forms of the 911-based concept car created a formal space for the future design of lines and details. But Porsche would not deviate from its formal path as rigorously as the concept car might have suggested. And it was still several years before the Boxster and 996 would premier, for example, before the lights could be recognized — with a little imagination — in series production. But the emphasized saucy hip swing could already be recognized in the 993. **And the eye-catching, candy-like colors immediately found their way onto the vehicle configuration list.**

Under the body with buggy-like open fenders, the 1989 technology of the current 911 generation operated with 250 hp and all-wheel drive. The head of development at the time (from 1988 to 1993) was Ulrich Bez. He was also previously with BMW, where he was responsible for the Z1, among other things. Interesting details included the roof opening, which would be found in the production version of the 993 targa, and the rims with two three-star elements apparently mounted on top of each other. **Two copies of this prototype were produced in Weissach.** Ferry Porsche received one as a gift for his 80th birthday. The company founder was not very enthusiastic, however. It had a bit too much of the current zeitgeist. And though a small series for the US market had been considered within the realm of the thought experiment, the high dollar exchange rate and the associated weakness in Porsche's sales thwarted such plans. Angst was the prevailing attitude in Zuffenhausen at the time.

#Prepared for a brawl

#Relic of days past

#The targa's final hour seemed to come in 1993. The targa-style roll bar had become outmoded. Convertibles had long ago done away with it, and a wide array of them were completely topless. And in the event of an accident, windscreen frames made of high-strength steels and, increasingly, retractable roll bars coupled with rollover sensors provided the necessary occupant protection. What still fit harmoniously into the overall picture of the predecessor — thanks to the rear panoramic window in the 1960s and '70s it was in fact quite en vogue — seemed almost a foreign body in the early '90s in the 964, with its more voluminous bumpers. And with a Cabriolet in the model range whose roof could be opened electrically for maximum convenience, the targa roof, which was fiddly and cumbersome to fold together and stow and was also acoustically problematic, was a relic from a bygone time. A total of just under 5,000 customers (3,534 Carrera 4, 1,329 Carrera 2) opted for the 911 with the matte black anodized roll bar, which was almost DM 6,000 more expensive than the Coupé. In terms of price, the Cabriolet, at DM 132,450 or DM 145,100, respectively (Carrera 2/ Carrera 4, 1992) once again ranked exactly DM 10,000 above the targa formerly offered as a safer Cabriolet. **It would be ten years before Porsche remembered the targa and offered it in a newly interpreted form.** And the roll bar didn't enter the scene again until the calendar showed 2014.

In 1991, assembly of a 911 took a total of 120 hours. After Porsche modernized its production processes, assembly time had dropped to 95 hours by 1993.

Speed Yellow

Porsche 911 Carrera 4 targa (964), 1989
Minichamps; Hockenheimring

Porsche 911 Carrera RS (964), 1992
Minichamps; Hamburg

Polar Silver Metallic

#Long live sports

#Despite all the improvements in driving safety, following the premiere of the Carrera 4, dynamic sports car enthusiasts missed the agility of the purist rear-wheel drive. And this not only because of the extra weight caused by the Cardan shaft, front differential gear and drive shafts, but also because of the nature of the all-wheel-drive vehicle, which is closer to understeering. **Porsche consequently added the Carrera 2 rear-wheel drive to the 1990 model year.** Technically, the 3.6-liter engine with double ignition and 250 hp remained the same. But for the competitors within the 911 community, that was not the last word. In those years, the subject of sport was a bit out of balance. The great years of the almost unbeatable Group C 956 and 962 racers in factory and private use were almost past, the 911s in GT use rather the hobby of committed private parties, the Formula 1 remake with footwork arrows an unusually unsuccessful undertaking. Factory sport was conducted with the transaxle 4-cylinder, the 944 turbo. In a brand trophy with which the company from 1986 onwards intended to promote the performance of emission control technologies, such as the regulated exhaust catalytic converter made of metal. After four years of racing, the front-engined Gran Turismo had seen its better days in the Cup. Porsche replaced the 944 turbo Cup with the Carrera Cup at the beginning of the 1990 season, thus establishing a tradition that continues to this day and is very much alive in numerous supra-regional and national Carrera Cups worldwide.

As a sports car, the 911, generation 964, was equipped with aerodynamically shaped rear-view mirrors and attractive five-spoke, 17-inch magnesium wheels. These Cup insignia immediately found their way into the series. **The Carrera RS sat a full four centimeters lower on the road, delivered 10 hp more and at the same time weighed about two hundred pounds less than its comfort-oriented sibling.** The main components of the weight reduction were the magnesium rims, an aluminum trunk lid and the absence of underbody protection and insulating material. The driver also had to dispense with electrically adjustable mirrors, sunroofs, heated rear windows or servo-assisted steering. Installation of a roll cage was planned from the outset for this — and would become a tradition for this most sportiest of all respective 911s. A total of 2,279 units were produced in 1990 and 1991, which Porsche offered for DM 145,450. In addition to the road-worthy Touring variant, Porsche also appealed to its motorsport customers with a Cup version and a Carrera RS prepared as a base vehicle for the GT-N racing class, i.e. further streamlined.

#Attractive horn section

#The next generation of the supercharged 911 appeared with a slight delay in 1990. Visually, it was new from the start. And the chassis, including the new 17-inch aluminum rims in Cup design, also documented the model change. Under the hood, however, a proven engine was at work. And following a discreet boost in performance, the familiar 3.3-liter engine put out 320 hp. Two years later, 360 hp were produced from the depths of the voluminous 3.6 liters of displacement.

The car immediately found admirers at the press presentation organized by Jürgen Pippig, then head of product press in southern France. Not only was the press enthusiastic, but so was the underworld: **Six of the 20 press test cars were stolen from the hotel garage at night.** The new price of the 911 turbo 3.6 of DM 204,000, which for the first time exceeded DM 200,000, made this theft a million-dollar one.

Between the appearance of the 964 turbo 3.3 and 3.6, the Porsche Executive Board also adapted the model future of the house and decided that everything would be different from now on: The foundation stones for the 986 (Boxster) and 996, the generation after next of the 911, were laid. With water cooling. The 964 generation, on the other hand, continued to rely on air cooling and the traditional body-in-white structure of the original 911.

Polar Silver Metallic

Porsche 911 turbo 3.6 (964), 1993
Minichamps; Herzogenaurach

Porsche 911 Carrera RS 3.8 (964), 1991
Atlas Collection; Bad Doberan

Cadmium Yellow

#Evolution of the aspirated engine

#At first glance, the 3.8-liter came across as the turbo S Lightweight, with puffed cheeks, aerodynamic cup mirrors, shiny, three-piece 18-inch aluminum rims and air intakes for brake cooling instead of the fog lights usually fitted next to the indicator lights on the 964. **It was ultimately the more voluminous, two-level rear spoiler which gave it away as a 911.** "RS 3.8" appears on the side covers of the screw connections of the upper, sixfold adjustable rear spoiler part. And this represented the most enormous displacement of the 6-cylinder engine to date, which with 300 hp now achieved as much as the turbo 3.3 did in the past. Only the Carrera RS 3.8 does not employ any turbocharging. Like the 260 hp 3.6-liter Carrera RS, its more powerful sibling has a direct connection to racing, which is what the abbreviation RS stands for. But as is typical for Porsche — that was not enough. The RS 3.8 (together with its even more uncompromising racing sibling, the RSR 3.8) was built in Porsche Motorsport department facilities on the development site in Weissach. It served as a base vehicle for homologating a competitor in the then-popular GT Cup, as well as other GT events like the 24 Hours of Le Mans. It promptly racked up its first class win there in 1993.

With thin glass windshields, two leather sports bucket seats, aluminum doors and hoods, front brakes from the turbo and rear brakes from the Carrera Cup model, without insulating material and rear seats, electric windows, power steering, radio and air conditioning, the most sportiest of all 964s weighs 1,249 kg. **With that it takes 5.2 seconds to sprint from a standstill to 100 km/h and can reach a maximum of 271 km/h.** The expansive body stands in the way, in the truest sense of the word, of achieving higher speeds. And while we're on the subject of technical data: The maximum torque of the 3.8 was 360 Nm; the official fuel consumption in combined driving was 15.3 liters. The price tag for this showed DM 225,000. A total of 55 units of the Carrera 3.8 RS were produced. In addition to the 35 cleared RSRs, this added up to a total of 90 cars. To be allowed to start the ADAC GT Cup, the engine power of the RSRs used in the race had to be reduced by 25 hp with the aid of an air restrictor.

#Live-cell therapy for the turbo

#The turbo marked the top of the range for many years, until Porsche identified this model as worthy of being expanded and made more powerful. **That time had come with the third generation 911: Above the "normal" turbo, Porsche placed the turbo S 3.6 Lightweight.** Under the hood, a 3.6-liter engine with double ignition and 381 hp was at work. The tail fin was a distinguishing mark. Like the hoods and doors, it was made of carbon, a material that was still exotic in automotive engineering in 1992. This brought weight advantages but also has its price. Porsche calculated DM 295,000 at the time for one of the 86 turbo S Lightweight cars produced. 25 years later, collectors pay up to EUR 1,422,960 to own one (at a Gooding auction in 2018). But other exotic 964s also fetch millions, like the Carrera RS 3.8 and Carrera RSR 3.8. **At an auction by RM Sotheby — also in spring 2018 — those models brought in EUR 1.34 million and EUR 1.025 million, respectively.** They are all painted in the then-popular cadmium yellow and drive on three-piece light alloy rims from the Italian company Speedline. With an 18-inch diameter and 8-inch width in front and 10-inch width in back. The tire widths are 235/40x18 and 265/35x18, respectively.

Cadmium Yellow

Porsche 911 turbo S Lightweight (964), 1992
Minichamps; Hamburg-Blankenese

#"Cars have made us independent for 100 years. One makes us dependent," was the title of the advertisement for the anniversary model of the 911 in 1993. Big headlines and bold colors were the style of the new campaign by the freshly selected creative agency Jung von Matt. Bold colors were also a striking feature of the model range at the beginning of the '90s. Under the direction of chief designer Harm Lagaaij, the zeitgeist — in an environmentally friendly and water-soluble form — was sprayed onto the car bodies. Names of the fashionable paint shades included Raspberry Red Metallic, Star Ruby, Violet Blue Metallic, Amazon Green Pearl Color, Dragonfly Turquoise Metallic, Riviera Blue and Iris Blue Pearl Color Metallic. The color of most anniversary edition 911s is Viola Metallic (with an interior in Rubicon) — it appears dark and noble, gleaming purple in the sun. And the gleam is accentuated by the lavish curves of this special 911, which wore the factory turbo look with a body that was 12 cm wider. The flared fenders intensified the already seductive light reflections on its sheet metal shell. **The special "30 years of 911" model was allowed to go without the tail fin of the turbo.** It was also able to pull it off, because — like (almost) all naturally aspirated 964s — it also has the electrically extendable spoiler. Starting at a speed of 80 km/h, it automatically stretched towards the sky. Or at the push of a button. Simply because you want to do it, or to ensure that police officers can't use the "aerodynamic driving stability aid" as involuntary proof of a possible speeding offense. M096 was the order number for the special model that was limited to 911 units. Historians count only 896 vehicles produced in the model years 1993 and 1994 — its successor, after all, had already been unveiled. **The price for the anniversary edition was DM 145,900.**

#Declaration of dependence

Viola Metallic

Porsche 911 "30 Years of the 911" (964), 1993
Minichamps; Niederndorf

#Generation III (964) and Panamericana

Porsche 911 Carrera 4 (964), 1989

Porsche 911 Carrera 4 targa (964), 1990

Porsche 911 Carrera 2 Cabriolet (964), 1989

Porsche Panamericana, 1989

#Generation III (964) and Panamericana

Porsche 911 Carrera RS 3.8 (964), 1992

Porsche 911 Carrera RS (964), 1992

Porsche 911 "30 years 911" (964), 1993

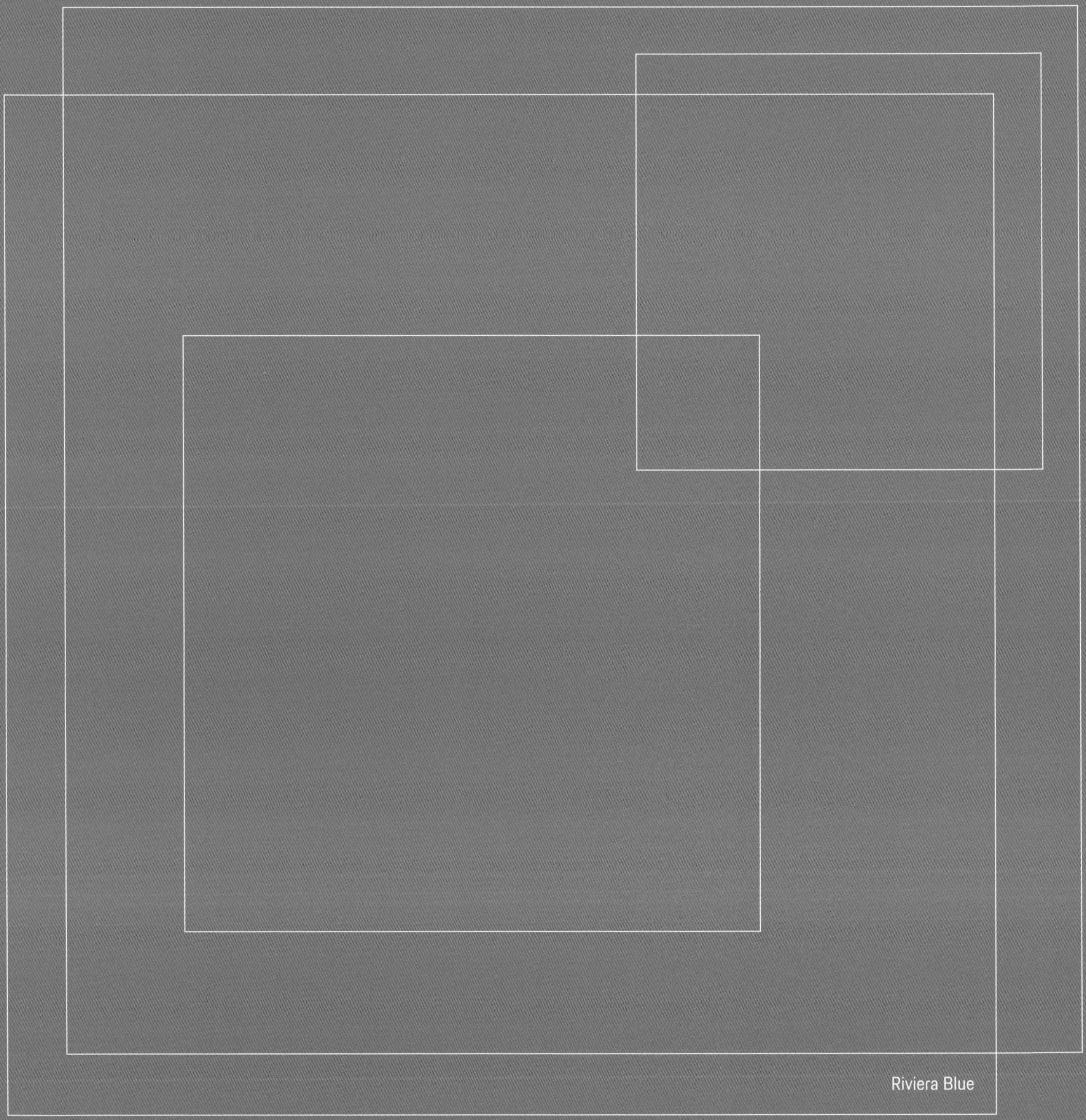
Riviera Blue

#Generation IV

(993) and 911 GT1

Porsche 911 Carrera (993), 1993
Minichamps; Hamburg

Arctic Silver Metallic

#The best is the enemy of the good, as they say. With the fourth generation of the 911 introduced in 1993 — 30 years after the exhibition premiere of the first 911 — its power and performance were increasing. Displacement remained untouchable at 3,600 cc. But instead of 250 hp, the pistons now lifted the crankshaft with the power of 272 hp thanks to revised engine insignia and a two-stage resonance intake system. **That's about 10 percent more power with around 5 percent less fuel consumption.** But that alone did not do justice to the new 911, which at the time was regarded not only in Zuffenhausen as the best 911 ever. While the chassis was still based on continued development of the original model, and the 901, 911 and 964 could also be recognized by laymen as closely related vehicles, product developers were required to do extensive work on the body in the project, running under code number 993. The flatter design of the fenders was based on the appearance of the 959 supercar as well as a family resemblance to the 968 and 928 Transaxle models, without forgoing the "sight lines" — the standing headlights — that were always so prized by Ferry Porsche. Modern polyellipsoid headlamp technology made it possible — along with brighter light. The front windscreen was glued in, which benefited the aerodynamics and acoustics. The rear continued to be adorned with a continuous strip of lights, but grew in width and concealed an all-new multi-link rear axle design. Thanks to better aerodynamics and increased performance, the 911 now accelerated to 270 km/h. That made a sixth gear necessary. In addition to the manual 6-speed transmission, the Tiptronic, an automatic introduced previously on the 964 that could also be shifted manually using toggle switches on the steering wheel, can also be ordered a surcharge of nearly DM 7,000. It was highly appreciated by comfort-oriented customers. As with its predecessor, the car could be requested with all-wheel or rear-wheel drive. It thus also retained the familiar nomenclature 911 Carrera 4 or Carrera 2, respectively. The four-wheel drive vehicles released after 1994 can be visually identified by white indicator lights in the front and red in the rear. Porsche charged DM 125,760 in the first model year for the manual rear-wheel drive.

Porsche proudly declared that not a single component of the new generation — with the exception of the logo — was identical to that of the 1963 911. The marketing copy read: "Over the years we have broken with many conventions — but never with our principles. That's why we believe that the sports car of the future is a classic one. And that it will honor its predecessors." The truth of this statement, made in the cheerfully colorful brochure, has long been confirmed. **The last air-cooled 911 is without doubt one of the most sought-after classics.**

And not only did the customer benefit from the extensive work done on the 993, but Porsche also rewarded itself with more efficient and thus more cost-effective production than for the 964, which featured many complicated and costly details. The multi-disc clutch, which carried expensive service costs, is just one example.

And it was clear from the outset that the 993 — unlike the initial assessment of the 964 — would be a 911 for the time being, since Porsche's head of development, Horst Marchart, had already given the go-ahead in 1991 for constructing a completely new 911 from the bottom up, including a new engine.

#911% fascination

#When the right hand knows what the left is doing

#Porsche presented the 993 generation, based on the body shell of the classic 911, at the IAA '93. The new Cabriolet followed in the spring. It was the immodest goal of the engineers to build the most perfect and beautiful 911 of all time while also preserving its origins. **In fact, the changes to the body are so extensive that the "new Carrera" appears to be a new vehicle.** Flatter fenders and visual elements borrowed from the 959 rejuvenate the front. Bulky rear fenders provide space for modern technology like a two-pipe exhaust system that permitting compliance with which the stricter legal requirements regarding noise and exhaust emissions. But anyone who has climbed into the interior quickly feels at home. And yet there are also once again innovations that cause the die-hard fan community to howl. For example, the new wind deflector that also opens automatically when the soft top is opened — electrically, of course — and makes the interior significantly less drafty. The new generation 911 proves to be an immediate hit. **Since 1970, no launch of a new model has been as successful as that of the 993 generation.**

Porsche was quoted in the brochure at the time: "Incidentally: As an exception, we dispense with teamwork in engine construction. **One mechanic assembles an entire engine — from start to finish.** So the right hand knows what the left is doing." As always, Porsche was also seeking the maximum that could be achieved with the 993. The air-cooled 3.6-liter boxer with Varioram intake system offered an increase in power to 285 hp for a surcharge of DM 12,850. For the final model year 1997, the new injection system, larger valves and variable intake duct lengths — and thus 285 hp — was series-produced for the 911 Carrera.

In the mid-'90s — the mobile phone had just begun its triumphal march and was becoming affordable — the 911's standard equipment included preparations for mobile phones and a remote-controlled central locking system.

The 993 was the last 911 with standing pedals. A relic from the automotive past. But for Porsche fans, it was also a matter of faith that is discussed as seriously as it was vigorously for the next generation of the 911.

Incidentally, at that point it took only 76 hours to build a 993 generation 911. This gave Porsche economic freedom for sustainable steps towards the future.

Raspberry Red

Porsche 911 Carrera Cabriolet (993), 1994
Minichamps; Baden-Baden

#The naked gun

#In terms of noise reduction and driving comfort, the RS of the 993 generation shamelessly copied its predecessor. In other words: no underbody protection, a largely uncluttered interior, no vibration damping measures in the drivetrain, electric windows, radio, airbags and central locking, but with a roll bar. Power steering and ABS — capable of use on racetracks, of course — had meanwhile become mandatory technical details even for high-performance vehicles. **And the 993 Carrera RS was capable of high performance, as the cubic capacity of the 6-cylinder boxer had grown from 3.6 to 3.8 liters.** Together with the new Varioram system with variable intake pipes, power output was increased to 300 hp. One could say that with the appearance of the 993 Carrera RS, the engine from the rather limited 964 Carrera RS 3.8 had found its way into series production. With a quantity of 1,014 units produced, however, the definition of series production could certainly be debated...

The fact that so few of this model — compared to the 964 — could be found on the racetrack was mainly because, with the spoiler-equipped Carrera RS 3.8 in the aerodynamically complete Clubsport trim or Cup trim, the RSR 3.8 as well as GT2, Porsche offered even more powerful base cars for fierce GT Sport competition.

Speed Yellow

Porsche 911 Carrera RS Clubsport (993), 1995
Minichamps; Kühlungsborn

Porsche 911 turbo (993), 1995
Minichamps; Erlangen

Arctic Silver Metallic

#The Porsche 911 turbo of the 993 generation is actually the reincarnation of the 959 in series production. But it is unlimited, a bit more mature in every way — and therefore better — and almost affordable compared to the supercar that at the time cost DM 420,000. The price list shows the 408 PS and 540 Nm all-wheel drive 911 with twin turbo 3.6-liter boxer for DM 212,040. Despite its remarkable performance, the newest engine development proved astonishingly low in exhaust emissions and in the mid-1990s was considered the world's lowest-emission car engine. In a worldwide first, all 911 turbo cars were delivered with the Onboard Diagnosis II — OBD II — with which emissions can be monitored by the vehicle control system and which was initially mandatory only for the US. Power-hungry customers could, if desired, also be served with performance enhancements. 430 hp is available with the WLS1. The second stage of development — as introduced in 1995, marking the end of the 911 air-cooled era with the turbo S — attains 450 hp.

The new supercar celebrated its premiere at the Geneva Salon in spring '95, but before it reached the customer it is already well into the second half of the year and, according to Porsche nomenclature, belongs to the 1996 model year.

In addition to the large, fixed, yet harmoniously integrated rear spoiler, the increase in the width of the car was especially noticeable. As with the 959, standard permanent all-wheel drive ensured maximum traction and driving safety. Also new were the 18-inch wheels with hollow spokes. This improved both the stiffness and the weight of the wheel. Behind the five spokes was a brake system suitable for the racetrack.

The new supercar was advertised in America without any complicated listing of its product features. The simple phrase shown on the ad for the 911 turbo there: **"Kills bugs fast."** The small print showed the power output and acceleration values. Including the summary: "Really bad news for the insect world."

#Series sibling of the limited super racer

#In the mid-'90s, GT sport celebrated a new heyday at Le Mans and other racetracks around the world that eventually grew into the popular BPR series — **the acronym stands for its three founding fathers Jürgen Barth, Patrick Peter and Stephane Ratel** — and even into a GT World Championship, awarded a rating by the FIA. The GT1 sports cars, according to GT1 regulations, were at its top as racing cars. The sports car category developed in record time from supercars formerly intended for street use like the McLaren F1 GT and Ferrari F40 into thoroughbred GT1 racers. But more about that elsewhere. Below the GT1 class, representatives of the GT2 category race against each other. An extremely attractive base car for this is the 911, among others, of which Porsche specially produced a homologation model in the 993 generation for racing: the 911 GT2. It was a turbo but had to get by without the standard four-wheel drive. In return, the developers in Weissach gave it full-grown wings, a comprehensive weight-loss treatment and bolt-on fender extensions that made room for even wider tires. In race trim, the GT2 delivered 450 hp. The street version required for the homologation still offered a robust 430 hp that would increase to 450 hp for the last two dozen street-legal GT2s at the end of its production period in model year 1998.

Press photos of an early GT2 for the street reveal that the new top model was originally meant to be marketed as a GT — or at least that's how it appears on the hood. But by the time the 911 GT1 appeared, the GT2 designation was set. It was later joined by the naturally aspirated GT3 based on the water-cooled 996.

#Thoroughbred and temperamental

Guards Red

Porsche 911 GT2 (993), 1995
Minichamps; Autostadt Wolfsburg

#View from the crystal ball

#At the 1995 IAA, Porsche announced the return of the targa, which was delivered to customers in 1996. This returned the range of body styles to the extent it was long known for. **The 993 targa was designed on the basis of the Cabriolet body, which was fitted with additional roof struts.** This made possible strikingly delicate C-pillars. The rather unloved Panamericana, presented six years earlier in Frankfurt, offered a preview of the architecture of the new roof. Instead of the once-cumbersome folding roof between the windscreen frame and the roll bar, which had to be dismantled, the new interpretation of the targa concept had a continuous glass roof from the front to the rear window. It can be opened electronically. When open, the upper part slid under the rear window. This allowed both light and air to enter the interior. But the sun could also be blocked by means of a roller blind. The first generation of this new form of targa was offered exclusively as a rear-wheel drive. It was popular from the start: **In some cases, the targa even outsold its closed-top sibling.** In 1995 and `96 there were almost 900 units of each; in 1997, with 1,833 units, there were in fact twice as many of the 993 targa.

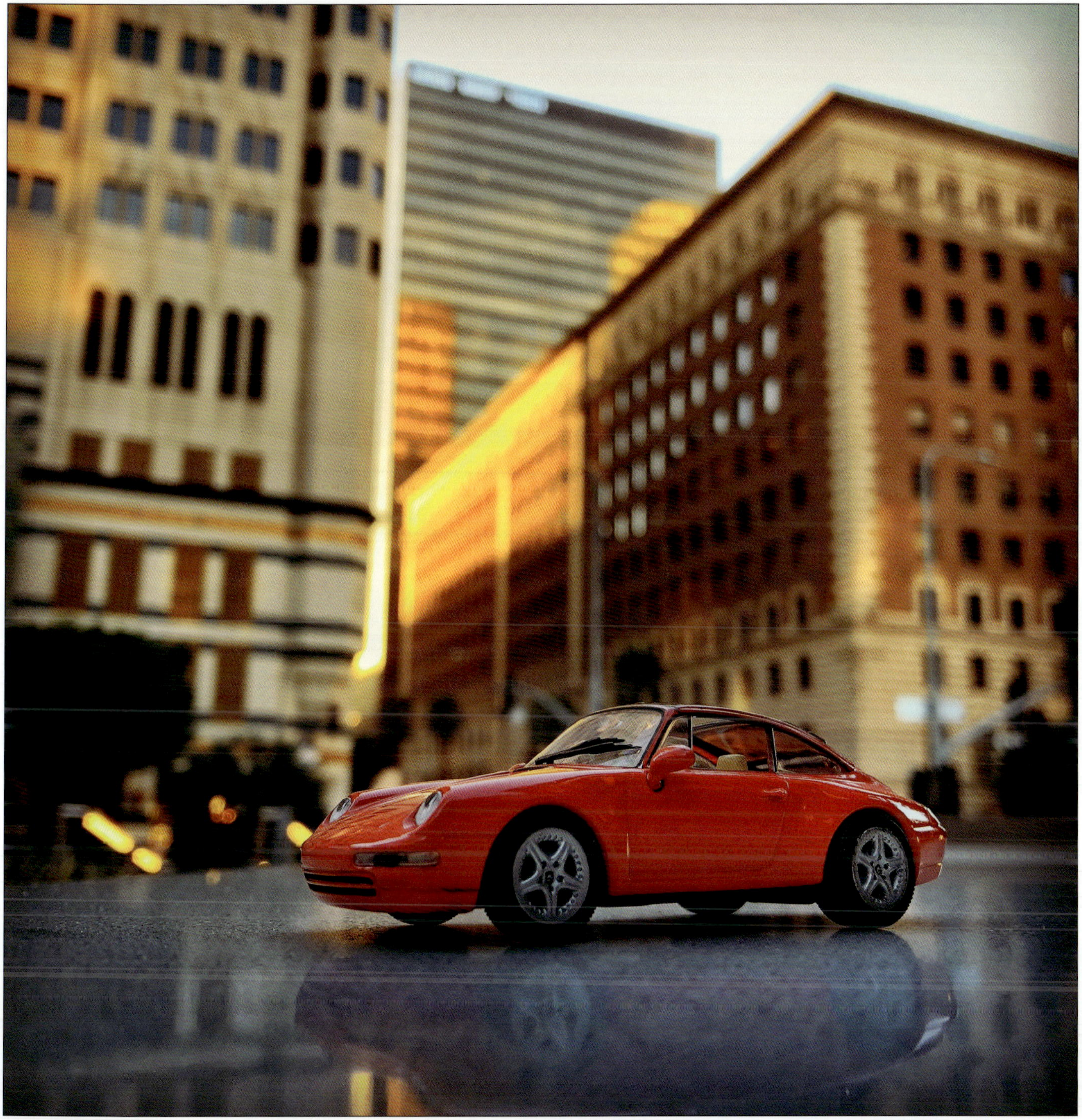

Guards Red

Porsche 911 Carrera targa (993), 1995
Minichamps; Herzogenaurach

Porsche 911 turbo Cabriolet (993), 1995
Schuco PRO.R43; Schloss Gabelhofen

Iris Blue Pearl Metallic

#Special requests by the dozen

#In the mid-'90s, Porsche fulfilled the wishes of a small group of 911 turbo Cabriolet fans who were actually waiting in vain for a successor to the open-top model. **With the help of Porsche Exclusive, 14 convertible turbo models were created of the 993 generation were created.** These were not pure 993 turbos, however, because the selected customers had to do without the wide turbo body and — even more importantly — the intelligent all-wheel drive. Instead, the Exclusive department took the 911 Carrera Cabriolet as its basis, furnished it with the 360 hp rear drivetrain of the 3.6-liter turbo, as was used before in the 964, and the exclusive small-scale production model was ready. It was, however, allowed to wear the turbo spoiler — the intercooler had to be housed somewhere... Viewed this way, it is actually a small-scale production 911 Cabriolet turbo instead of a 911 turbo Cabriolet. But that would be splitting hairs.

#A complete success

#"Seam and surface, curve and edge, aggressiveness and softness, strength and elegance, speed and steadfastness, focused concentration and playful casualness: forces that seem to strive in opposition, balanced in precise suspension" — that was how Porsche itself tried to interpret the 911 phenomenon. The American actor, comedian, author and ardent Porsche fan Jerry Seinfeld summed it up this way: **"Most high-end sports cars remind me of Halloween costumes: these are monster masks for their drivers, as if they were designed for Cirque du Soleil. A Porsche feels like a warm, round pebble in your hand."** And he's not alone in that opinion. The harmonious design of the 911 is mesmerizing from the start. Perhaps a bit more with some models. The Carrera 4S and Carrera S of the 993 generation certainly belong to the latter group.

In the fourth generation of the 911, Porsche also recalled its success with the "factory turbo look" and offered the Carrera — the naturally aspirated version of the 911 — with the broad-shouldered, rounded fenders originally reserved for the turbo. The scope of delivery also includes lavish 18-inch wheels. The Carrera 4S introduced in 1995 and its rear-engined sibling Carrera S, which was added a year later, forgo the fixed wing mechanism of the double-charged power pack. In terms of engine, the S models are identical to the Carrera, meaning both have the air-cooled 3.6-liter boxer with 272 hp, or, in model year 1997, 285 hp.

In addition to the lettering on the hood, the two-part ventilation grille in the extendable rear spoiler of the Carrera S serves as a visible distinguishing feature between the all-wheel and rear-wheel drive models. It is reminiscent of the Porsche 356 Carrera 2, whose round back also features two ventilation openings.

After some years that had been rather mixed, Porsche was now back on the road to economic success. In 1995, the 911 found twice as many customers as before. With 3,714 units produced, the Carrera S remained a thoroughly exclusive derivative of the series. But the models with which the brand was starting to outpace others were already at an advanced stage of development. Considered this way, the term 'complete success' also applied to the company.

Arctic Silver Metallic

Porsche 911 Carrera S (993), 1996
Schuco; Lake Geneva

Porsche 911 turbo S; 993, 1998
Minichamps; Buxheim

Riviera Blue

#Last curtain call for the air-cooled engine

#At the end of the '90s, Porsche offered turbo customers larger superchargers, a correspondingly adapted engine control unit as well as a more generously dimensioned oil cooler for a surcharge of DM 29,800. The bottom line is a 10 percent increase in power output and a rated output of 450 hp. This increase in factory output became the core of the 911 turbo S, offered starting in 1998, which marked the evolutionary peak of all road sports cars with air-cooled 6-cylinder boxers. **It is the last curtain call for the era of the air-cooled 911.** Visually the turbo S can be identified by the extended aerodynamic package (Aerokit II), that is, the two-level rear spoiler, and the air intake openings in the upper part of the rear fenders. The latter have been familiar to brand connoisseurs since the 959.

Not only the power is remarkable, but so is the corresponding torque of 585 Nm. The sprint from 0 to 100 km/h is completed in just 4.1 seconds — which is faster than this sentence can be read. Only at a speed of 300 km/h do performance, driving resistance and air resistance balance each other out. According to the standard cycle, fuel consumption is 13.2 liters of premium gasoline per 100 km. In comparison, two decades later, a 580 hp 911 turbo S of the 991 generation uses only 9.1 liters for the identical distance.
At the end of the nineties, Porsche produced a total of 345 911 turbo S models. In 2018, the anniversary year, another 450 hp 993 turbo would be built just in time for the "Racing Reunion" event in Laguna Seca. Project Gold used parts from the Porsche Classic squad.

The golden yellow car was assembled from over 6,500 original spare parts and a body-in-white that was also in stock. The unique specimen was not granted street-legal status, however, as there was no historical chassis number for the redeveloped body. That scarcely bothered the collector who bought the vehicle at the end of October for EUR 2.7 million for the benefit of the Ferry Porsche Foundation. Arguably the most noble of all 993 turbos will hardly become a "daily driver" during its lifetime.

#A wanderer between worlds

#In the mid-'90s, after one and a half decades of impressive racing battles, the era of the Group C prototypes ended. Excessive costs and a corresponding decline in interest on the part of car manufacturers involved in this category meant the end of the excitement on the track — as is so often the case in motorsports. Previously, the highly developed factory racers had robbed the professional individuals and racing teams of their chances of success. Too expensive, no competition and no spectators; time for something new. The sports car experts Jürgen Barth, Patrick Peter and Stephane Ratel founded the BPR series. Here, street-legal sports cars were entitled to start. And with powerful exotics such as the McLaren F1, Ferrari F40, Venturi, Morgan +8 or the Porsche 911 GT2, there was a range of suitable sports cars. The series promptly boomed. But the usual motorsport mechanisms are also used here: The manufacturers quickly developed their own sports cars that complied with the letter of the regulations. In the case of the GT1 regulations, this meant at least one street-legal version had to exist. In reality, however, these showpieces with number plates represent full-blooded racing cars. This was also the case at Porsche, where the 911 GT1 was built in the Porsche Motorsport department for the 1996 racing season. And it was a hybrid not only in terms of its intended use — its structure is actually taken from two vehicles: The front end and floor assembly come directly from the 993 generation production 911, but the rear end with the drivetrain comes from the 962 C. **Inside, a grid mesh with flattened roof protects the driver. And on top is a feather-light carbon body with an impressive rear spoiler.** The first 911 with mid-engine was complete. Unlike its competitor, Porsche produced a total of 23 street versions of this GT1 sports car with a 3.2-liter 6-cylinder engine and 544 hp. With heating, a horn, light and exhaust catalytic converters, it had everything German Road Traffic Licensing Regulations (StVZO) specified for homologation. In fact, the cars, weighing just 1,120 kilo and with speeds up to 310 km/h are hardly seen on the road and have disappeared into the garages of collectors. **With a price of DM 1.55 million, the homologation vehicle was priced quite highly.** But even the price is governed by the regulations. For the '97 season, the look and aerodynamics of the 911 GT1 were adapted to those of the 996, which had meanwhile been introduced. And a completely new car followed for the '98 season. But that deserves its own story.

Speaking of mid-engine 911s: For the 2017 racing season, Porsche GT race director Frank-Steffen Walliser once again put a mid-engine 911 on wheels. The Porsche construction kit makes it possible for the 4-liter 911 RSR to achieve a weight distribution suitable for racing — with the help of chassis parts from the 718 Cayman.

Seal Grey Metallic

Porsche 911 GT1 96; 1996
Minichamps; Brooklyn

#Token car

#For the GT series, which now was being held as a World Championship, Porsche Motorsport put a thoroughbred racing car on the wheels that actually had nothing left in common with the standard Porsche 911 — apart, perhaps, from the headlights and taillights. But it also answered to the GT1 abbreviation that stood for the racing class. And to ensure that everything was proper, the homologation of the racing car also included a street-legal variant, as required by the regulations. Unlike the previous namesake, whose chassis was based on the steel bodyshell of the production 911, the structure of the 98 911 GT1 was made entirely of carbon fiber. **The '98 model did not have much in common with the 911 GT1 of the same name that was shown two years earlier:** The implementation was uncompromisingly trimmed for racing use, which helped to noticeably cut the weight of the sports car even further. The five competition cars produced — used by the factory and the Zakspeed team — each weighed just 950 kg. Their top speed was 330 km/h.

On the hilly track of Road Atlanta — and not only there — the aerodynamically sophisticated mid-engine GT1 911s temporarily lost their footing and frightened both drivers and spectators by involuntarily taking flight. **But at Le Mans, just in time for Porsche's 50th anniversary, the factory cars presented the assembled audience with a first- and second-place victory** — against extremely strong competition from Toyota, Nissan, BMW, Mercedes-Benz and the rest.

Snow White

Porsche 911 GT1 98; 1998
Onyx; Göttingen

Porsche 911 Carrera (993), 1993

Porsche 911 Carrera Cabriolet (993), 1994

Porsche 911 Carrera RS (993), 1995

Porsche 911 GT2 (993), 1995

Porsche 911 turbo 3.6 (993), 1995

Porsche 911 turbo Cabriolet (993), 1995

Porsche 911 Carrera Targa (993), 1995

#Generation IV (993) and 911 GT1

Porsche 911 Carrera S (993), 1996

Porsche 911 GT1 (98), 1998

Porsche 911 GT1 street (96), 1996

Porsche 911 turbo S (993 WLS II), 1998

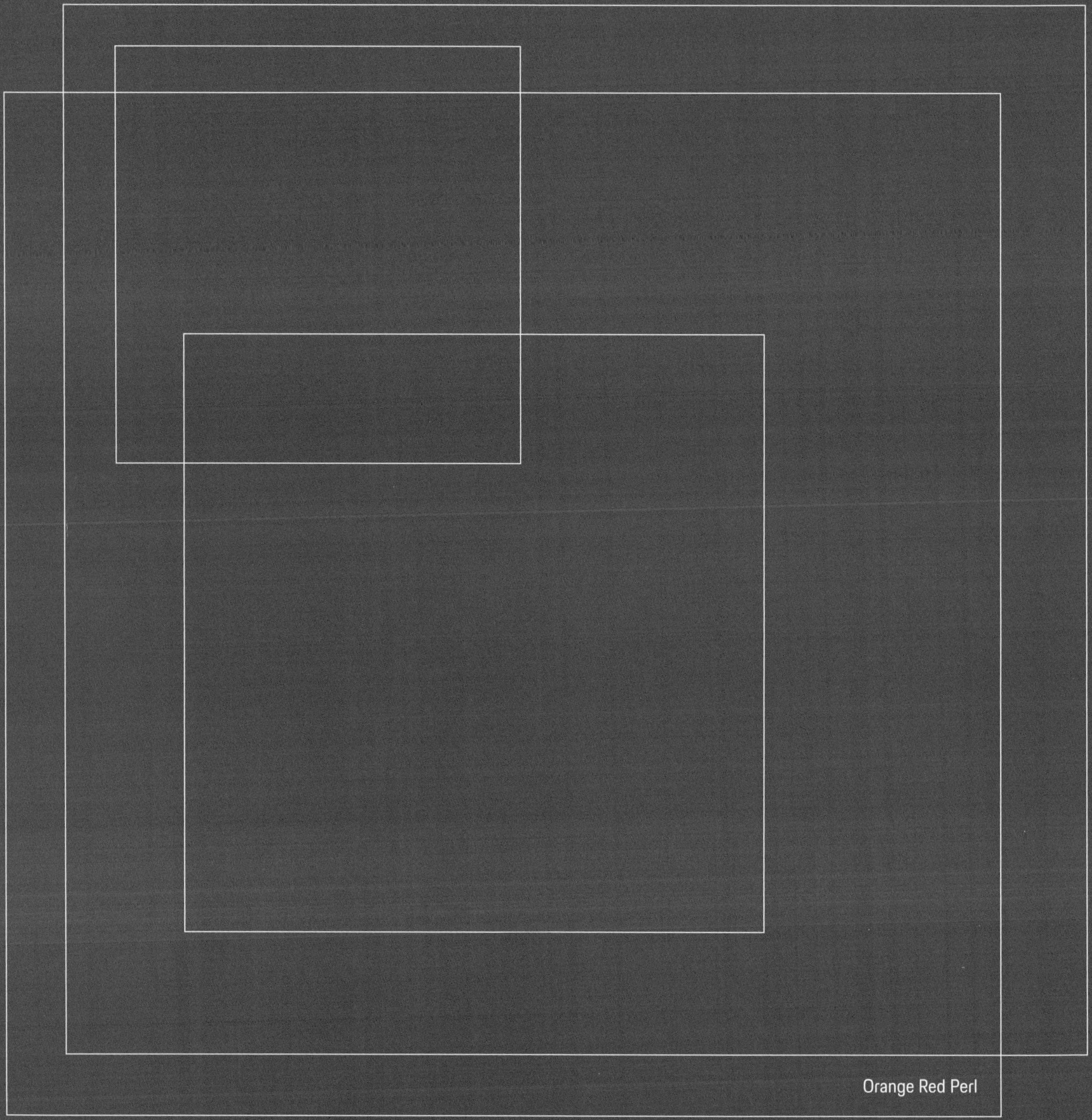

Orange Red Perl

#Generation V

(996)

Porsche 911 Carrera (996/I), 1997
Schuco; Herzogenaurach

Paladio Metallic

#Whispers were spreading through the fan community: With the latest 911 generation coming two years after the Boxster, the completely redesigned icon of the model range appears, bearing the model code 996. And it appears to be the spitting image of the Boxster, which is positioned as a new entry-level model. A bit of sleight of hand, as the Boxster and 911 were using parts from the same shelves — a full half of their construction details were identical. For Porsche, this bit of artifice was essential for survival. Behind this were the concerns of men like former CEO Wendelin Wiedeking and head of development Horst Marchart. **The foundation stone for the new model range, which built on one another, was laid at the beginning of the '90s.** At the time the predecessor to the 996 — the 993 — was about to be launched on the market, Porsche was in deep water. There had been job cuts in Zuffenhausen and Weissach. Mercedes production orders — including those for the 500 E — were most welcome, and a takeover by Daimler-Benz was being discussed. The new boss streamlined the model range, the days of the Transaxle models were numbered, and the marketing strategy called for "full concentration on the brand core" — the 911. And with the Boxster, a sexy new model was created below it. Also with a 6-cylinder boxer and the aura of James Dean — or that of his 550 Spyder.

The new 911 grew in size and offered its occupants an unprecedented amount of space and comfort. Its slender flanks were a bit reminiscent of the early 911. In addition to Porsche Stability Management (PSM), new features included the Weissach interpretation of driving dynamics control (ESP), an on-board entertainment system with screen and a navigation system.

Of course, it would have been more adept at that time to let the Boxster follow the 996. But the still-young 993 was too fresh for that and, financially speaking, the Stuttgart-based company had no time to wait for the Boxster. The new generation of water-cooled engines was yet another milestone in the minds of the die-hard fan community. Once and for all, the air-cooled boxer became obsolete at that point. But here, too, the people in Stuttgart had no choice as increasingly stringent emission laws required cleaner, more modern engines. The hood conceals a power package that can hardly be seen from the outside, with 3,347 cc displacement, 4-valve technology, "VarioCam" camshaft adjustment and 300 hp power output — but without the characteristic fan wheel it had for decades. This equals the performance capacity of a 911 3.3-liter turbo or 964 Carrera RS 3.8. In keeping with Porsche tradition, power output grows with product updates and the introduction of additional model variants. But that's another story — please just turn the page...

Almost 180,000 vehicles were produced by the end of the nine years of production for the fifth generation of the 911, from 1998 to 2006. Porsche needed 16 years, from autumn 1973 to summer 1989, for the almost 200,000 units of the second-generation 911.

#Paradigm shift with resistance

#Irish rain

#Peter Gutzmer was the project manager responsible for developing the new water-cooled sports car family. And the convertible version of the 996 had the potential to turn his hair gray. The reason was the watertightness of the top construction, which had to be suitable for high speeds. It passed with flying colors every conceivable test in climatic chambers, under laboratory conditions, driving through water, in everyday traffic and in every conceivable car wash. All's well if testing ends well. If it hadn't been for the comments by technical colleagues who noticed water penetrating during test drives in Ireland. At home in Weissach, the cars are meticulously examined and mistreated with steam-jet devices, as if they had to withstand tropical downpours. And they stayed dry inside. As well it should be for a soft top to which engineers have devoted their utmost attention. For the 996 generation, it was lined with sheet metal elements that made it quiet even at high speeds. **It could be opened and closed electronically in just 20 seconds. And it disappears — also automatically — under a rear roof flap.** This makes the cumbersome fumbling with a tarp that has to be unfastened by hand a thing of the past. Extensive stiffening measures increase the empty weight of the convertible 911 by 75 kg. Another 33 are added when the optional aluminum hardtop is attached. Part of the weight also comes at the expense of the standard roll bars, which extend explosively behind the rear seats in the event of a rollover. And in addition to the airbags for driver and front passenger in the steering wheel and instrument panel, side airbags are now also placed in the doors. Porsche charged almost DM 19,000 in 1998 for making the leap from Coupé to Cabriolet.

As far as the Irish rain was concerned, additional test drives on that North Sea island found that the rain occurring there had a different water quality which, in combination with the weather conditions sometimes prevailing there, allowed the damp water to migrate under the roof seals. **Error detected — error eliminated.** The rubber seals were promptly furnished with a new coating. And the 911 Cabriolet remained waterproof. Everywhere in the world.

Black

Porsche 911 Carrera Cabriolet (996/I), 1997
Minichamps; Walting

#Always surefooted

Shortly after the convertible version, Porsche began offering the all-wheel-drive Carrera 4 again in autumn 1998. It was shown on the price list at DM 147,640, ranking it nearly DM 11,000 more than the rear-drive Carrera 2. Customers got a comfortable sports car that was always easy to handle with qualifications for long drives and trips. **The 996 measured 20 cm longer than its predecessor, the 993.** Passengers were the primary beneficiaries of this added space. Critics felt reminded more of the 928 than of the classic 911 in terms of space and comfort. But as a precaution in case of an accident, the safety zones are also more generous than those of the predecessor. The luggage compartment was also more spacious. All 996s shared new instrumentation. That was also cause for excitement among the "Gusseisernen" (the cast iron ones), as the inveterate community of fans of the air-cooled 911 likes to be called: Instead of the five individually installed round instruments with the tachometer in the middle, the first liquid-cooled 911 now featured a collection of instruments that merged all five round instruments into one. Visually, the new set of instruments looked as if the five round instruments had been pushed into each other; practically, as if two semicircles on the left and two semicircles on the right were now gathered around the tachometer, which was still in the middle. **There was also a digital speed display.** Another new component is the Porsche Communication Management (PCM) located in the center console, with a screen. It contained a navigation system, on-board computer, hands-free telephone and (still at that time) a cassette radio.

The Carrera 4 had all-wheel drive with a Visco clutch system, as had already proved impressive in its predecessor. **New features included drive-by-wire gas pedal, ABS and Porsche Stability Management.** From 1999, Porsche's interpretation of ESP was also available for rear-wheel drive 911 models. Experts identify the all-wheel-drive vehicle by the front indicators in a transparent white look. This also put an end to the teasing about looking like a "fried egg." On request the white indicators are also available for the Carrera 2. They quickly became a standard accessory.

Cobalt Blue

Porsche 911 Carrera 4 (996/I), 1998
Schuco; Brussels

Porsche 911 GT3 (996/I), 1999
Minichamps; Herzogenaurach

Lapis Blue Metallic

#Long live sports — on the streets as well

#Porsche once again chose the Geneva Salon in March — something like the official start of the European automotive year — to present a model. **In 1999, it was the 911 GT3, the first series-produced Porsche approved for street use, that cracked the mystical 300 mark — with a top speed of 302 km/h.** The slim 911 with slightly flared rear fenders and an eye-catching yet elegant wing mechanism is a sibling in the spirit of the Carrera RS 2.7. Its visual attributes included characteristic 18-inch spoke rims that hid red brake calipers, being 30 mm lower and having light side skirts. With the abbreviation GT3, it joined the pecking order below GT1 and GT2, the racing classes popular at the time. And the GT3 category is also equipped from the outset with genetics that are suitable for use on the racetrack. Its first event is the Porsche Supercup, which is held as part of Formula 1 events. But the GT3 also quickly became the sports car of the numerous national Carrera Cups and Club Sport events. The GT3 also proved to be an ideal tool in long-distance sports such as those regularly held on the Nürburgring's Nordschleife.

Its engine is based on the crankcase of a formerly air-cooled engine block, with roots in the 962 and 911 GT1 racing sports cars. **In the GT3, the water-cooled engine has a displacement of 3.6 liters and mobilizes 360 hp.** With it, the two-seater racer sprints from 0 to 100 km/h in 4.8 seconds. At the start, Porsche planned for 1,350 units of the DM 179,500 911 GT3. But sales of these cars was so high that the sports car manufacturer produced more. In total, 1,868 GT3 of the first series of the 996 were produced in the 1999 and 2000 model years, plus 508 vehicles for 2001. That makes grand total of 2,376 of the first GT3 series. They prepared the ground for a top competitor within the 911 family that is still successful today.

#Car lovers already got a preview of the turbo in its 996 garb at the IAA 1997. But friends of the top model in the series would have to wait until mid-2000 before the water-cooled version of the supercharged sports car was ready for delivery. **The flared, bulbous fenders celebrated their comeback with the turbo.** All-wheel drive had been obligatory for the most powerful representatives of the 911 class since the 959 and 993 turbo. With 420 hp as standard, the performance level is almost as high as that of the supercar 959. The racer's stoppers were also impressive: a lavishly dimensioned brake system with red painted calipers peeked out from behind the 18-inch wheels. From the end of 2000, even more powerful brakes would be added to Porsche's traditionally extensive list of extras: For a surcharge of DM 15,000 there was a Ceramic Compound Brake — race-tested, extremely durable and guaranteed not to fade even at the most brutal pace. Experts recognize it by the look of the disc surface; laymen by the yellow paint on the brake calipers. The base price for the turbo Coupé was DM 237,250 — on the same level, technically and otherwise, with the mid-engine 8-cylinder engines from Ferrari. **The new variable valve control system called VarioCam Plus came as standard.** It included a camshaft adjustment with additional switchable bucket tappets. Also new were the front headlights with newly shaped fog lights. After just a few years, the 911 had regained its familiar appearance with the characteristic round headlamps. **A 5-speed automatic transmission — called Porsche Tiptronic S — was now also available as an option for the turbo.** What had been an exceptional competitor thus became a highly positioned luxury glider with exceptional performance. Customers overseas were not the only ones to appreciate this...

#Gran Turismo par excellence

White

Porsche 996 turbo, 2000
Minichamps; New York City

#Arrived in the here and now

#For the model year 2002, the voices of critics against water cooling had long since fallen silent. **The 996 has long been recognized as the fifth generation of the 911, and the oft-criticized "fried eggs" are a thing of the past.** The fog lamps remain part of the lighting units but their appearance was once again rounder and therefore closer to the original face. The new face celebrated its premiere with the turbo but became standard for all of the professionally face-lifted 996 generation 911s — and this time the term facelift hit the nail on the head. But the redesigned 911 didn't just look better: thanks to Bi-Xenon, the occupants also see better at night. The glove compartment now available was also helpful. Progress in airbag development had made this possible, as had the introduction of side airbags. However, the model update measures of the second series of the 996, which were hidden under the sheet steel body, were much more far-reaching. The engine in particular was attracting a great deal of attention: While the water-cooled boxer number one still measured a total combustion chamber volume of 3,387 cc, the cubic capacity increased to 3,596 cc from the 2002 model year onwards. **The initial 300 hp will be increased by another 20 hp for the model update.** The comfortable 911 now runs at 285 km/h instead of 280 km/h as a manual. And the sales documents show fuel consumption as 11.1 liters of fuel per 100 km. As powerful and silky smooth as the rather young 4-valve unit might have been, it frequently attracted negative attention in the early years due to a leaky crankshaft seal on the transmission side. This resulted in labor-intensive service measures. This was good for those who regularly had their Porsches serviced in the Porsche Center. Porsche rewarded consistently stamped service booklets with good treatment. And since model year 2005, a double lip shaft seal has prevented any incontinence by the engine. This also settled that issue once and for all. For the brand, the introduction of the water-cooled 911 was a big and important step. **In the end, with over 175,000 units, three times as many of the 996 vehicles were produced as its predecessor 993.** This opened the door for Porsche to today's size.

Guards Red

Porsche 911 Carrera (996/II), 2001
Minichamps; Herzogenaurach

Porsche 911 GT2 (996/II), 2001
Minichamps; Nuremberg Airport

Meridian Metallic

#No compromises

#Porsche opened its first dealership in Beijing in mid-2001. From then on, the Chinese could also order a Porsche. For Porsche, the move into the "Middle Kingdom" was the beginning of a successful liaison; over the next few years, China would ultimately develop into the sports car manufacturer's largest sales market.

The 911 GT2, the 996 version of the model formerly developed for motorsport homologation purposes, also appeared in 2001. This GT2 was again a turbo, which came without four-wheel drive — as was mandatory for most motorsport applications Further modifications to the sports car, which was limited to 500 units, included the Porsche ceramic composite brake, two more powerful turbochargers and a weight-loss treatment that — compared to the turbo — melted off a full 100 kg. The scale now showed 1,440 kg. The ceramic brake alone saved 18 kg compared to its steel counterpart. And a sporty ABS was also included in the scope of delivery.

The flagship of the model range was listed at DM 339,000, or EUR 173,328. The model family also boasted top performance (462 hp) and driving performance: Only at 315 km/h do propulsion and driving resistances balance each other out. The sprint from a standing start to country road speed was achieved in just 4.2 seconds. For effortless passing maneuvers, the powerful 620 Nm torque also proves to be an advantage. In comparison, its 320 hp 3.6-liter naturally aspirated sibling still had a respectable 370 Nm on the crankshaft.

The new aerodynamics met the increased cooling requirements of the powerful engine. The air that brought the middle radiator, or the coolant conducted through it, to acceptable temperatures flowed out through an opening in the upper part of the front bumper, directly in front of the trunk lid. The air, on the other hand, was guided through the side radiators and directed outwards via the front wheel arches. Below the rear wing, modified intercoolers and an intake air-collecting storage box collect the incoming air. Dry sump lubrication suitable for motorsport with an 11-liter oil reservoir was also standard.

Porsche 911 Carrera targa (996/II), 2001
Minichamps; Ehrwald

Arctic Silver Metallic

#Under glass

#The brochure for the 2002 model year confidently described the second generation of the 996 as the successor to the first 996 and thus indicated seven evolutionary stages — including the 959 — of the 6-cylinder Boxer icon. "Passion 911" was the title of the sales documents, which also tell the story of the 911 at the Targa Florio, the legendary race held on Sicilian roads that Porsche won eleven times, not counting numerous class victories. Targa had also been chosen as the key point because the open-top variant that ranges between the Coupé and Cabriolet was once again part of the model range. As with the 993, the targa had an electrically opening glass roof that could be opened from front to rear. When open it was stored in a space below the rear window, which on the targa could now be opened like a tailgate — making it extremely practical.

Behind it was the traditional space for the engine, which, with the advent of water cooling, was also hidden from curious glances when the engine hood was open. **Technically, the 3.6-liter light metal boxer was one of the finest.** Even without turbocharging, VarioCam Plus, a two-stage resonance suction system and an electronic engine management system (Motronic ME 7.8) adapted to the electric (drive-by-wire) gas pedal, the (still optional) PSM and all engine parameters (Motronic ME 7.8) are standard features. Tiptronic S already had a delivery share of 36 percent.

#Traditionalists were delighted with the return of the continuous red lighting strip that had been a permanent feature of the 911 since 1973 but had disappeared from the scene with the appearance of the 996. But the red strip was back with the introduction of the Carrera 4S, starting from the 2002 model year.

#Loyal gang

And drivers of naturally aspirated engines could once again enjoy the rounded cheeks of the turbo wide body. The curve of its hips was 44 mm wider. And there were parallels to the turbo under the body: All-wheel drive and the turbo brake system were standard. **At that time, one in three 911s was ordered with four-wheel drive**, including the TipTronic option. This automatic transmission now had five gears. Starting in spring 2003, Carrera 4S and turbo were also available as convertibles.

Guards Red

Porsche 911 Carrera 4S Cabriolet (996/II), 2003
Minichamps; Schwabach

#Germany's next top model

#The turbo Cabriolet was a top model popular with customers and dealers alike. They couldn't get enough of this car — literally, as availability was an issue. Those who nevertheless gained possession of one enjoyed 420 hp, which could also be upgraded to 450 hp by increasing the factory power output. But no matter which performance class the customer chose, the turbo engine block was based, like the GT3, on the block originally used in the air-cooled 911 and the 911 GT1. Dry sump oil lubrication was obligatory and ensured that the life-preserving lubricating film for the engine is never cut off, even in the most active driving style with the highest transverse and longitudinal acceleration forces.

With the appearance of the turbo S starting in 2004, the performance boost previously listed as an extra now entered series production. The surcharge of around 13,500 was comparatively moderate as the ceramic brake system and an audio system with CD changer were part of the standard delivery package of the turbo S — produced in Coupé and Cabriolet form in Zuffenhausen.

Black

Porsche 911 turbo Cabriolet (996), 2003
Minichamps; Nuremberg

Porsche 911 GT3 RS (996/II), 2003
AutoArt; Berlin Tempelhof

Cararra White/Red

#Renaissance of the RS

#2002 marked the birth of the 996 GT3 RS. As with its ideal predecessor, the Carrera 2.7 RS, the letters R and S arranged next to each other stand for "racing sport." And quite rightly so, since the RS had its origins in the Porsche Motorsport Department located on the edge of the Porsche Development and Testing Center in Weissach, at the town limits of the Flacht municipality. The father of the vehicle was the racing and development engineer Roland Kussmaul, who at the time wanted the 911 GT3 steering knuckles used in racing to help reduce tire wear on the 911, which sat very low in racing mode. **As a result, a homologation model of the face-lifted 996 generation of the GT3 was brought to maturity and conceived for 200 units — initially under the radar of the Board of Management.** New rims, visually similar to the traditional Fuchs rims, and a color scheme in Carrera White with a choice of red or blue trim, as well as lettering in "Danube waves" style, add details that recall the Carrera 2.7 RS and captivate fans. **A total of 682 units were produced in 2003 and 2004, 200 of them with the blue regalia.** Under the hood was a 3.6-liter boxer, homologated at 381 hp, but it actually produced over 400 hp on the crankshaft, as all first-generation GT3 RS models have performance-enhancing polished combustion chambers. Compared to the normal GT3, the GT3 RS was almost 50 kg lighter. Measures including the carbon-fiber trunk lid, mirror and rear spoiler, the use of a single-mass flywheel and reduced insulation measures cut 47 kg. In addition, the furnishings are covered for the first time in Alcantara, and — another first for Porsche — Pirelli P Zero Corsa brand sports tires are standard. With a total weight of less than 1.4 metric tons, good traction and a sporty 6-speed manual transmission, the rear-wheel drive unit with a maximum speed of 306 km/h accelerates from a standstill to 100 km/h in 4.4 seconds. Deceleration was provided by internally ventilated steel brake discs in the dimensions 350 mm (front) and 330 mm (rear), respectively. Racing-tuned ABS prevented tire damage due to hard braking. The price list in 2003 showed EUR 120,788. Fifteen years later, collectors of the GT3 RS happily pay double that.

#Generation V (996)

Porsche 911 Carrera (996/I), 1997

Porsche 911 Carrera Cabriolet (996/I), 1997

Porsche 911 Carrera 4 (996/I), 1998

Porsche 911 GT3 (996/I), 1999

Porsche 911 turbo (996), 2000

Porsche 911 Carrera (996/II), 2001

Porsche 911 GT2 (996/II), 2001

#Generation V (996)

Porsche 911 turbo Cabriolet (996/II), 2003

Porsche 911 Carrera targa (996/II), 2001

Porsche 911 Carrera 4S Cabriolet (996/II), 2003

Porsche 911 GT3 RS (996/II), 2003

Aqua Blue Metallic

#Generation VI

(997)

#With the premiere of the 911 with the type number 997, the sports car, now in its fifth decade, once again had round main headlights. Its seductive lines with gently curved hips — that is, harmoniously widened arched fenders — also met with high approval. Especially for the all-wheel models. **The design team at the time, under the leadership of Harm Lagaaij, included designers Grant Larson and Matthias Kulla.** They polished the 911 to perfection. Down to the smallest detail — including the new side mirrors, which not coincidentally are reminiscent of the Carrera GT supercar.

The "concert master" — that is, the person responsible for the 997 series — was August Achleitner. His task was to marshal the various disciplines for the new vehicle, from development and testing to production, and to also maintain an overview of the entire model family, since the Carrera is the 911 foundation on which Porsche has traditionally built other variants of the 911. In 2004, the sports car manufacturer asked sardonically: **"What can you make from a fascinating sports car?" And promptly answered: "Two!"** From the outset, with the appearance of the sixth 911 generation, Porsche offered the Carrera and Carrera S models, which differed in terms of engine power and performance.

While in the S versions of the 996 only the equipment, body width and price defined the differences between the Carrera and the Carrera S, in the 997 the models have different engines: The Carrera comes with 3,596 cc of displacement. The Carrera S breathes from 3,824 cc. This translated into 325 hp and 355 hp. Thus they were separated by 30 hp and at least EUR 10.000. Brand experts identify the Carrera S by its 19-inch wheels and the double-flow exhaust system. An extensive list of extras also gave Carrera buyers the opportunity to order other wheels and exhaust systems. It was also available with an increasingly popular valve exhaust, which plays a distinctive and concise concert at the push of a button.

Both engines were also available in combination with all-wheel drive as Carrera 4 or Carrera 4S. In combination with the three body styles Coupé, targa and Cabriolet, this added up to a dozen different 911s.

All in all, the 911 series in the 997 generation comes in two dozen variants, from the basic Carrera and the turbos to the various GT models; just barely street-legal or customized for various motorsport applications. August Achleitner remained the successful master of ceremonies for the 911 until entering a well-deserved retirement. His last big concert would be held in late 2018 with the appearance of the eighth generation 911, the 992.

#With a familiar face

Arctic Silver Metallic

Porsche 911 Carrera (997/I), 2004
Minichamps; Kühlungsborn

Porsche 911 Carrera S Cabriolet (997/I), 2004
Minichamps; Heiligendamm

Night Blue Metallic

#For every taste

#The rear-wheel drive Carrera and Carrera S roll off the production line with the "narrow" 1,808 mm wide body. Their all-wheel-drive sibling models, the Carrera 4 and Carrera 4S, are almost 5 cm wider — their width measures precisely 1,852 mm. They all shared the electrically extending rear spoiler, which, when closed, was used as a ventilation grille for the hood. **At a speed of 120 km/h, the component lifts upward.** The aerodynamics modified in this way provide additional directional stability at high speeds. At significantly lower speeds of up to 50 km/h, the convertible top can be opened or closed electrically. In the open state it primarily rests under the collar of the body.

#The development efforts of the engineers in Weissach have long focused not only on progressive perfection in terms of driving performance and environmental friendliness but also on the continuous evolution of assistance and entertainment systems. This included the new main instrument cluster, in which the five round instruments that had previously been forcefully pushed into each other were somewhat pulled apart, thus once again approaching the classic model.

Another new feature was Porsche Active Suspension Management (PASM), in which the driver could vary the shock absorber setting at the touch of a button. **The optional Sport-Chrono-Plus package could also be used to adjust the characteristics of the gas pedal curve.** The engine electronics delivered perfect intermediate throttle shocks during downshifting — for 911 drivers who haven't fully mastered the traditional heel-to-toe game or the dance with the outer edge of the right foot. Speaking of footwork: Porsche decided to dispense with the car jack and spare wheel in the 997 due to the ever-increasing size of wheels and tires, to the increasing scarcity of space resulting from numerous safety and environmental protection technologies, and to the weight of the vehicle. That saved 10 kilos of weight. In their place, there is a breakdown kit in the trunk.

#In step with the times

Basalt Black Metallic

Porsche 911 Carrera 4S (997/I), 2005
Minichamps; Big Sur

Porsche 911 turbo (997/I), 2005
Minichamps; Stuttgart-Zuffenhausen

GT Silver Metallic

#Big feet

#The 997 turbo was born at a time when Porsche could report one success story after another. In parallel to the sports cars, the Cayenne was enjoying great popularity, and the development of new markets in the East was proving to be a successful step. Once again — true to the motto "the best is the enemy of the good" — the latest 911 generation proved to be the best to date. This also applied to the turbo, which was first manufactured in Zuffenhausen in June 2005. Three months earlier, the very last turbo of the 996 generation left factory 2 in Zuffenhausen. The twin-turbocharged 3.6-liter engine now mobilized 480 hp. In addition there was a very strong 680 Nm of torque. The new turbochargers with variable loader blades are primarily responsible for the 30 hp increase in performance. At the same time, they have a highly beneficial effect on the responsiveness of the turbo engine. In Porsche-speak this is called VTG and stands for Variable Turbine Geometry. **The days of the "turbo-moment-of-hesitation" — the delayed, then abrupt power output — are long gone.** The maximum speed was 310 km/h and the average fuel consumption was 12.9 liters per 100 km. An international jury of 65 trade journalists honored the turbo engine in 2008 with the coveted and important **"Engine of the Year" award.** Porsche's then-CEO Wendelin Wiedeking was also on a turbocharged economic course: This was the time when the foundation stone was laid for finally bringing Porsche and Volkswagen back on track together.

#Everything except standing still

#Porsche wrote provocatively in one of its product catalogs: **"We don't believe in the myth of the perfect sports car. Otherwise, we would have stopped our work 45 years ago."** Indeed, the 911 knows about everything except standing still. This applies to the model itself as well as to individual variants. The transparent Targa roof with its slender roof racks began its third model generation with the appearance of the 997 Targa. The veil on the sixth generation Targa 911 was raised in December 2005. Thanks to new glass technology, the weight of the electrically opening glass roof was reduced by almost 2 kg. For the first time, the Targa — now capitalized — would be delivered only with four-wheel drive and a correspondingly wide body. The price list started at around EUR 94,000 for the Targa 4 and an additional EUR 10,000 for a Targa 4S. **Half a year later there was a power boost for the Targa 4S to 381 hp.**

Arctic Silver Metallic

Porsche 911 Targa 4S (997/I), 2005
Minichamps; Munich

#The pure doctrine

#This was how Porsche described the most powerful of all 911s. It refers to the 911 GT3 RS. Following positive experiences with the GT3 RS of the predecessor generation, the GT3 for the 997 was set from the beginning. The displacement of the racetrack-capable, naturally aspirated sports car remained at 3,600 cc, while the power output increased to 415 hp. **The car was furnished with everything it needed for fast and precise driving.** Superfluous bells and whistles were left off. The color palette was also reduced. But customers did not have to sacrifice anything in terms of driving performance and dynamics. In concrete terms this meant the GT3 RS weighed 20 kg less than the GT3 — despite its standard roll cage and slightly wider body. That was the result of the interplay of various materials. Various steels are used — including high-strength and ultra-high-strength steels, hot-formed (known as "tailored blanks") — as well as aluminum and carbon. While the hood and doors are made of light metal, the rear wing, inspired by the Cup version, was made of carbon fiber. The rear window was made of plastic — that alone saved 3 kg. The street-legal sports car with standard Clubsport package and chassis tuning specially optimized for circuit sprints from 0 to 100 km/h in 4.2 seconds. To ensure the vehicle comes to a stop promptly and effectively, a brake system with 6-piston aluminum brake calipers in monoblock construction and 350 mm brake discs (at the front axle; at the rear there are 4-piston brake calipers) together with sport-optimized ABS. An even more stable ceramic brake system, which was developed in racing to series maturity, is available on request. **For a surcharge the GT3 RS, which can reach a speed of 310 km/h, was available in orange or green.** Standard colors were either Arctic Silver Metallic or Black. In addition, contrasting orange mirrors and rims as well as a decorative stripe following the "Danube waves" of its ancestor, Carrera RS 2.7. The standard roll cage was also orange.

In 2010, a standard GT3 RS impressively demonstrated the razor-sharp implementation by Porsche engineers of the concept of a road-going sports car suitable for racing: Porsche provided a quartet of drivers with a standard car, with which the racing drivers commuted by car from Stuttgart to the Nürburgring, where they furnished the car with starting numbers, passed the technical inspection with no problems and then plunged into the racing action of the legendary 24-hour race at the Nürburgring. At the end of the chase they had gone through 3,680 race kilometers, two sets of front brake discs, another set of brake pads and 10.2 liters of fuel per lap. In the overall standings, the team of 180 starters finished in 13th place overall and then returned the car to Weissach on its own axles. The odometer showed: 4,594 km. The condition of the vehicle: Ready for more adventures. Very few are capable of that!

Arctic Silver Metallic/Orange

Porsche 911 GT3 RS (997/I), 2006
Minichamps; Barcelona

#A comprehensive model update was scheduled for the 2009 model year. This time the facelift for the 997 generation of the 911 was unusually extensive. The new front apron with daytime running lights using LED technology and the new almond-shaped LED rear lights are notable on first sight. The indicators and taillights were also implemented using energy-saving LED technology. The all-wheel versions now had a continuous red strip, reminiscent of the continuous band of light on the air-cooled 911s of generations two to four, and that can also be seen on the 911 Carrera 4S of the first water-cooled boxer generation.

More important, however, were the new technical features hidden under the body. More power output, lower fuel consumption and emissions — this was an eternal credo for the developers in Weissach. And this time they were taking a big step. The boxer engines were now equipped with direct fuel injection. In contrast to the previously installed intake-manifold fuel injection, the mixture formation now takes place entirely in the combustion chamber. This is good for fuel consumption, torque and power alike. Fuel consumption was reduced by up to 15 percent, and the performance of the 911 Carrera's basic 3,614 cc engine increased by 20 hp to 345 hp. The 3.8-liter engine of the 911 Carrera S even jumped from 355 hp to 385 hp.

Also new was the 7-speed dual-clutch transmission. It can be shifted manually or driven as an automatic. And it goes by the name PDK, which had already been introduced to the racetrack in the 1980s. This meant the days of the automatic known as Tiptronic (with torque converter) were numbered. The advantage of the PDK: It shifts free of any interruption of traction power, since a gear is always preselected with the dual clutch transmission. **The dual clutch practically shifts back and forth between two gears engaged in parallel.** With conventional transmissions, the gears first need to be sorted and selected when disengaged.

#The sustainable becomes even more sustainable

Macadamia Metallic

Porsche 911 Carrera (997/II), 2008
Minichamps; Pebble Beach

Porsche 911 Carrera 4S Cabriolet (997/II), 2009
Minichamps; Gaistal

Nordic Gold Metallic

#Open to enthusiasm

#The tight-fitting, electrically operated folding top with its magnesium substructure had achieved a level of perfection unrivaled in the cabriolet category. Even so, Porsche also offered an optional aluminum hardtop that was lined and soundproofed from the inside. **This also made the convertible 911 weather and winter-proof.** Especially when it came to the all-wheel version. In conjunction with Xenon headlights, the 911 also has cornering and bend lighting. Porsche Traction Management, or PTM for short, ensures maximum traction at all times on all-wheel drive models. It uses sensor data and computer control to distribute the drive power between the permanently driven front and rear axles with the aid of a centrally positioned multi-plate clutch. This means that 911 drivers can safely get up to speed on slippery roads or in record time. For those in a hurry, there is a tried and tested way to exploit maximum acceleration capacity: **All models with PDK gears have so-called launch control.** For the driver this means: Press the Sport-Plus button, shift to "D" or "M" position, left foot on the brake, press the gas pedal with your right foot, and then remove your left foot from barks and reaches. The engine barks, develops 6500 rpm. And off you go: The 911 accelerates as if shot from a cannon... In the case of a Carrera 4S Cabriolet, the stopwatch stops at 4.7 seconds when the speedometer reads 100 km/h, or 10.1 seconds when it reads 160 km/h. Also new was the "racetrack shift strategy" function. **It was designed for the shortest possible shifting times and optimum switching points.** For competitors who watch every single second, the stopwatch (part of the Sport Chrono Package Plus) is centered in the instrument panel, prominently in the field of vision.

#Over the years, the Targa has developed into the elegant and versatile Gran Turismo of the 911 model range. With standard all-wheel drive and customarily generously equipped, it appealed to a different clientele than a puristic Carrera or the "sharp knives" of a GT3 and GT3 RS. The elongated roof arches, accentuated with chrome, gave the Targa its unique, characteristic roof line. The rear window, which also acted as a tailgate, was an appreciated, practical detail of the Targa. It could also be conveniently opened with the car key's remote control. And thanks to the electric closing aid, it could be closed both effortlessly and safely. The wind deflector on the upper windscreen frame, which automatically extended when the roof is open, was another practical detail. It enabled draft-free driving with the top down, even at higher speeds. Another new feature, at least for PDK vehicles, was a drive-off assistant that helps to start off on hills without rolling or jerking. The system simply maintained the brake pressure for two seconds and released it again when the vehicle started up after sufficient starting torque had been built up.

The tastefully luxurious character of the car was also matched by the extensive range of desired colors and comfort extras. Electrically adjustable sports seats were as much a part of this as the leather available in various extents and numerous colors. Even the individual slats of the air conditioner outlets could be covered with tanned cow skin. The leather steering wheel, covered in interior color, was more or less the normal standard. In addition, there was the possibility of adding further accents with interior elements made of wood, carbon or aluminum look. Thanks to the extensive range of products on offer, hardly any 911 was like another.

#Coupé or Cabriolet? Both!

Malachite Green Metallic

Porsche 911 Targa 4 (997/II),
Minichamps; Siegburg Umland/Heiligendamm

Porsche 911 Carrera Sport Classic (997/II), 2009
Schuco; Tuchenbach

Sport Classic Grey

#An impressive EUR 201,682 was charged for the Carrera Sport Classic, which would be produced in 2010 in a 250cc edition based on a 911 Carrera S with 3.8 liters. **This exclusive 911 celebrated its premiere at the IAA 2009.** In fashionable gray — the specific name for the special color was Sport Classic Gray — with the ducktail reminiscent of the Carrera RS 2.7, 19-inch aluminum rims in the legendary Fuchs look, a 44 mm wider rear, ceramic brake discs and, thanks to a newly developed resonance intake system of the direct fuel injection engine, an increase in performance of 23 hp to 408 hp as well as a lavishly finished interior decorated with braided leather. **Another new feature was the roof over the occupants, which had additional curves — providing room for tall passengers to wear safety helmets.** Porsche would bring this detail in the sportiest of all the 911s of the 991 generation to series production. After the introduction of the electrically extending rear spoiler — with the 964 — the rear spoiler was actually no longer needed for aerodynamic reasons. But love of tradition brought it back to life.

A manageable number of units, careful handling of the company's tradition and a sure sense of style put the Carrera Sport Classic on the list of collectible 911 gems right from the start. **Accordingly, the notable additional charge of EUR 105,791 compared to a Carrera S is also put into perspective over time.** While the latter model today offers the possibility of acquiring a mature 911 at an attractive price — even with the high resale values usual for Porsche — the former model is traded at collector's conditions. Either way, a 911 always proves a good investment. And special specimens regularly prove to be an investment that guarantees a profit. This matches well with the fact that more than 70 percent of all Porsches ever produced are still in running order.

#Style references

#Fine individual products in series production

#Max Hoffman, a car dealer who emigrated from Austria to the USA, provided the idea for the Porsche 356 Speedster — the small, minimally equipped car that makes good money in America. **After the positive experiences that the company had in the late '80s (911) and early '90s (964) with the new editions of the Speedster concept, Porsche remembered this concept once again in 2010 and began producing a special series limited to 356 units.** The car was presented at the Paris Salon in October of the same year — the blue color of the exhibited car fit perfectly there.

Technically, it was a 911 Carrera GTS with a shortened windscreen and two arched fairings mounted behind the two bucket seats. The 3.8-liter 6-cylinder engine with direct injection mobilized 408 hp. This puts it in the same class as the Carrera Sport Classic, and it still delivers 23 hp more than the Carrera S. The transmission is a 7-speed PDK. Porsche Dual Clutch (PDK) was an indication that Porsche had developed this transmission technology in racing. Tight switching times without traction interruption ensured fast lap times (on the racetrack in the mid-1980s in the 962 C) and lower consumption on the road (since the facelift version of the 997 starting in 2008).

Another reference to an earlier style was the classic design of the five-spoke Fuchs aluminum wheels with black spokes and polished rims. But while they were a maximum 16 inches under the well rounded fenders on the 911 of the first two generations, the sixth generation 911 bore large 19-inch wheels with rear tires in the generous 305 format. The body grew accordingly by 4.5 cm in width. The doors and front hood were made of aluminum.

As with its recent and older predecessors, the simple Speedster roof meant doing without certain things in terms of suitability in bad weather. Doing without also applied to the choice of color: The 2010 Speedster was available exclusively in Carrera White or Pure Blue. They all feature a black bezel around the headlights. The weight saved in the doors and hood was balanced out with extra comforts such as a Bose sound system, telephone, navigation, parking assistant and Sport Chrono Plus package. The surcharge compared to a GTS was EUR 50,000: The price for the Speedster, which was sold out at breakneck speed, was EUR 201,682. But the increase in value of the limited two-seater has also delighted its buyers. **The 911 Carrera Sport Classic had already proved a great success the year before.** From that perspective, Porsche was not the only one to give itself a gift to mark the 25th anniversary of the special order specialists at Porsche Exclusive Manufaktur.

Pure Blue

Porsche 911 Speedster (997/II), 2010
Atlas; New York City

Porsche 911 GT2 RS (997/II), 2009
Minichamps; Schloß Bensberg

Guards Red/Carbon

#For a fast lap

#At the time of its introduction, the GT2 RS with 620 hp was the most powerful street Porsche of all time. Its twin-turbocharged 6-cylinder boxer delivered 8 hp more than the Carrera GT's V10, which was developed directly from racing.

The rear-wheel-drive "racing" derivative intended for the road — or collector's garage — and generously trimmed for lightweight construction with visible carbon would be presented at the Moscow Motor Show. This was to be understood as an expression of appreciation for Russian customers who preferred the Cayenne Turbo S in everyday use, which sometimes involved challenging traffic on Russia's roads. In any case, the series, limited to 500 copies, was already sold out during the exhibition. At the unit price of EUR 237,578 and to all countries of the world.

Porsche had already laid the foundation stone for the GT2 RS in 2007 when Walter Röhrl was rampaging over the Nordschleife with a lightened and slightly more powerful GT2. In Porsche engineering circles, the 560 hp development car went by the name "Lighty" and with it, the rally ace was five seconds faster from the get-go than with the "standard" GT2. The GT2 Nürburgring record lap in 2006 — which took just 7:32 minutes — was already a sensation since it was on a par with the lap of the supercar Carrera GT, which was originally designed as a racing car. New on the GT2 was the customized Porsche Stability Management (PSM) including stability and traction control that could be deactivated at the touch of a button.

The standard GT2 mobilized 530 hp from its supercharged 3.6-liter 6-cylinder engine. That was enough for 3.7 seconds (0-100 km/h) and 329 km/h. The figures for the 620 hp GT2 RS were 3.5 seconds and 330 hp — the maximum speed was electronically controlled. **And the GT2 RS takes just 7:18 minutes to complete a lap on the Nürburgring's Nordschleife...**

#Ferry Porsche summed it up: **"The 911 is the only car you can drive from an African safari to Le Mans, then to the theater and finally on the streets of New York."** With the 356 in 1948, the son of designer Ferdinand Porsche laid the foundation stone for the brand that today puts more than a quarter of a million sports cars on the road every year. He set the course for the future, transforming production from a hand-built construction process to series production. When he died 50 years after the premiere of the first Porsche — the two-seater mid-engine roadster — Porsche had once again won Le Mans. And the era of the air-cooled 911 came to an end with the 450 hp all-wheel drive 911-turbo-S of the 993 generation. The success of the 911 continued, and Ferry Porsche's statement continued to be true for the following decades. Though the company's founder did not live to see the 997 series turbo S, this model proved the versatility of this unique sports car more impressively than ever. With all-wheel drive, a long list of technologies for safety and comfort and a healthy dose of power output, packed in a highly functional yet attractive body shell, this 911 is also a car for all occasions. **Sales of the 997 as a turbo were launched in 2006.** The basic engine with a smooth 3,600 cc displacement was quite familiar. The turbo now features 480 hp and the turbo S presented in mid-2007 has a full 530 hp — just as the GT2 had prior to that.

#For all occasions

Ice Blue Metallic

Porsche 911 turbo S (997/II), 2007
Minichamps; Barcelona

#Generation VI (997)

Porsche 911 Carrera (997/I), 2004

Porsche 911 Carrera S Cabriolet (997/I), 2004

Porsche 911 Carrera 4S (997/I), 2005

Porsche 911 turbo (997/I), 2005

Porsche 911 Targa 4S (997/I), 2005

Porsche 911 GT3 RS (997/I), 2006

Porsche 911 Carrera S (997/II), 2008

Porsche 911 Targa 4 (997/II), 2008

Porsche 911 Carrera Sport Classic (997/II), 2009

Porsche 911 Carrera 4S Cabriolet (997/II), 2008

Porsche 911 turbo S (997/II), 2010

Porsche 911 Carrera Speedster (997/II), 2010

Porsche 911 turbo S (997/II), 2010

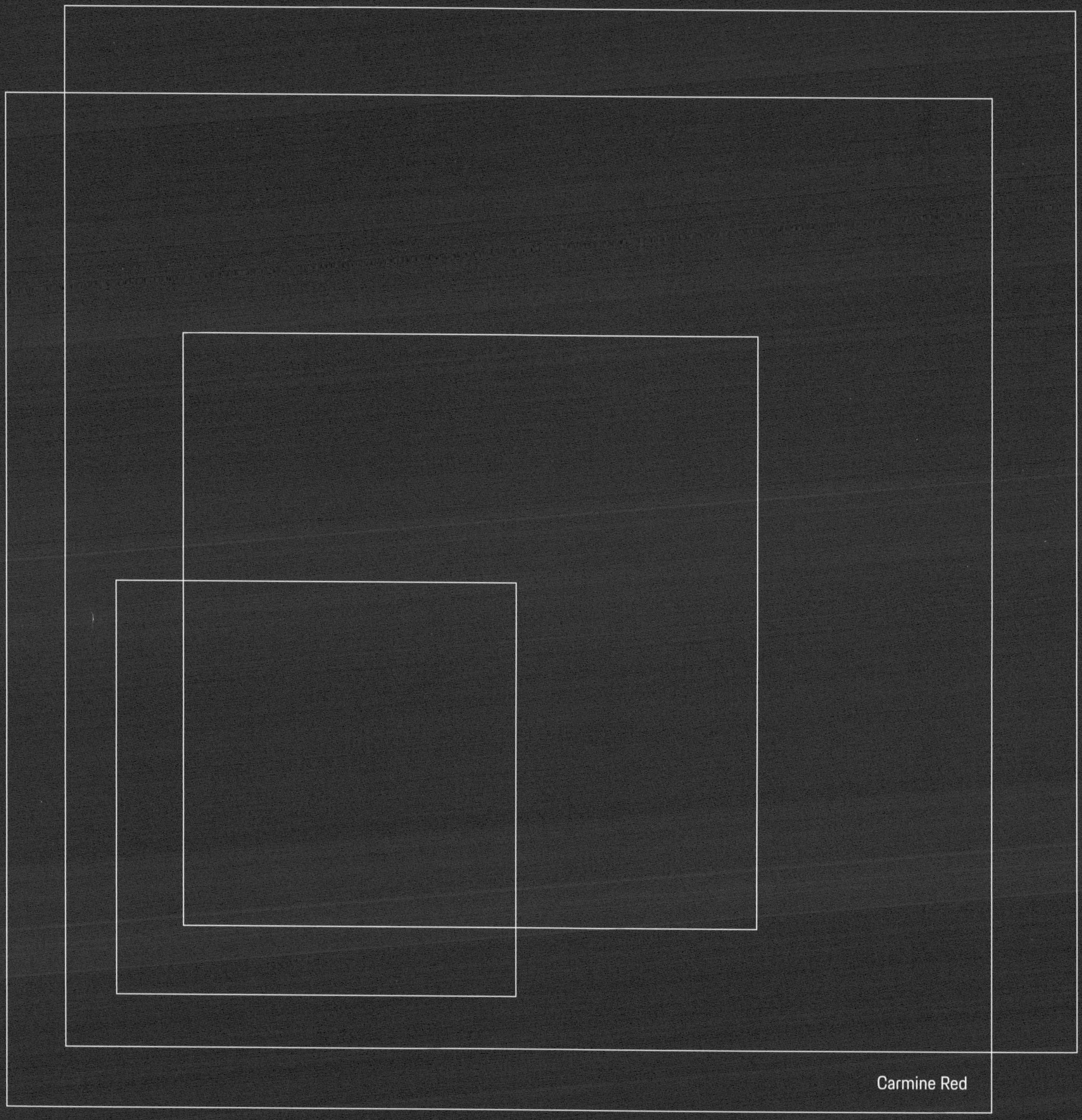
Carmine Red

#Generation VII

(991)

Porsche 911 Carrera (991/I), 2011
Minichamps; Paris

Agate Grey Metallic

#A new era

#In September 2011, the seventh generation of the 911 celebrated its exhibition premiere in Frankfurt. **Porsche was slowly running out of 900 digits and the 911 was given the model series code 991.** It was the first generation of the 911 to be built with people in Wolfsburg having a say. Porsche AG, after tough negotiations between Porsche CEO Wendelin Wiedeking and Volkswagen Supervisory Board Chairman Ferdinand K. Piëch, became part of the Volkswagen Group in 2012. Before that happened, Wiedeking, who had taken Porsche to previously unknown heights, bowed out of the company in summer 2009: He made way for the former Porsche Production Board Member Michael Macht, who led the Executive Board temporarily before moving to Wolfsburg in mid-2010 and handing over management of Porsche to Matthias Müller.

For the day-to-day business of the product developers, the involvement of Wolfsburg also means additional coordination loops. As a result, the design of the latest generation of 911s, which had in large part already been approved, was slightly modified once again, with proportions being changed minimally and the design of the front headlight covers being made to look like those of the 917.

Michael Mauer, who came from Saab, had been Porsche's head of design since 2004. Over the years he had developed a harmonious, distinctive yet traditional design language for the sports car manufacturer. His work — and the resignation of Volkswagen's top management around Martin Winterkorn, who was felled by the diesel affair — would result in his promotion to head of design for the Group in 2015. During the development phase of the 991, however, it was still viewed critically by his predecessor, Walter de Silva, then head of design for the Volkswagen Group, as well as by then-CEO Martin Winterkorn. And "Salzburg" — the nickname within the Group for Supervisory Board Chairman Ferdinand K. Piëch, who was always involved and well-informed — always had some important things to say. The small tweaks they made are not indicative of a particular need of improvement, but rather represent a desire to make a contribution, however small. Technically, the new basis now featured a 350 hp 3.4-liter engine. The diversified model policy with various engines and power levels, drive and body types has proven its worth. **Things remain the same in this respect, but a new age had long since dawned for Porsche.**

#Tradition and future

#Porsche described the timelessness of the 911 in its brochure with succinct words: "Tradition. Future." This might indeed successfully describe the essence of the 911 — the automotive focus and spiritual anchor of the brand. After all, each new generation embodies both the origins and the future. **Each 911 generation stands independently, appears to be a logical consequence of further development of this model, that at the same time appears eternally timeless.** Every 911 parked next to a current 911 — regardless of age — can be identified without doubt as a typical 911. By anyone. "Not a single piece of today's 911 is identical to its 1960s counterpart. Yet the essence of our iconic sports car has remained the same. For more than 50 years," said Wolfgang Porsche.

Evolution instead of revolution. Always one step better. That's the way Porsche has always considered it. Everything new and yet with an unmistakable identity. **And the identity of the 911 was fixed at various points: Clearly, its design is what preoccupies many people. In many ways.** Whether on the playground, at the regulars' table, or on a scientific level. For example, the German Design Council, which was founded after the premiere of the 991 under the title "Pleasure or burden? The design of an icon" dealt with the challenges the design of the 911 presents for its designers. Does the tradition of the 911 lead to a dead end, or can the great theme continuously be reinterpreted? For Ferdinand Alexander Porsche, creator of the original 911 and founder of the successful Porsche Design label, the seventh generation of the 911 was the last he would experience. "Butzi" Porsche died in April 2012 at the age of 76. He did not live long enough to accept the distinguished Red Dot Award.

The success of the 911 was not just a formal issue. Its complex nature was yet another of its strengths: "A Porsche is always exclusive but is also suitable for everyday use. This also expresses a down-to-earth attitude," Wolfgang Porsche said. **"Porsche customers don't just want to get from A to B; they want to live and love these sports cars."**

And the seventh generation of the 911 also experiences love and passion. The basic model with 3,436 cc of displacement stood from the outset alongside the more powerful S model with 400 hp from a smooth 3,800 cc. After their premiere at the IAA 2011, the first vehicles would be introduced on the market or in customer hands in early 2012. And in the Porsche Museum, which opened in 2009 and is well worth seeing both inside and out, the brand dedicated an exhibition presenting all seven generations. Its title: Identity 911.

Cognac Metallic

Porsche 911 Carrera S (991/I), 2011
Minichamps; Paris

Porsche 911 Carrera S Cabriolet (991/I), 2012
Minichamps; Barcelona

White

#With a short delay, and in time for the spring sun, Porsche released the convertible version of the rear-wheel drive 911 in the two engine variants. **The Cabriolet top construction was once again ingenious.** With the help of three lightweight yet stable magnesium elements, the hood was stretched taut over the two plus two occupants when closed. Porsche engineers call them convertible top arches. These reduced wind noise and fuel consumption. **The drag coefficient cW measured — as with the Coupé — just 0.30.** Standard with the lined, electrically operated roof was a heated glass rear window. The roof could be opened and closed within 13 seconds. And also while driving up to 50 km/h. The Z-shaped fold protects the inside of the roof from dirt. The wind deflector, which was also installed as a practical bit of standard equipment behind the rear seat, protects against uncomfortable turbulence in the interior. It was also electrically operated — within two seconds and at speeds up to 120. The rear spoiler extends electrically already at 80 km/h. On the 991 this, rather than the grille element, was the rear end section below the trunk lid, which has been cut even shorter and has long since become a refill opening for operating fluids — the engine could no longer be seen, even when the trunk lid is open.

A further detail of the Cabriolet are the two roll bars hidden behind the rear seats, which extend explosively in a fraction of a second in the event of a rollover and thus offer the occupants of the open-top car a safety space. Passengers in the front seats are also protected in an emergency by six airbags — as in all eleven cars since the 997.

And to ensure the comfort of Porsche drivers even when the sun is not shining, the developers also devoted great attention to winter and bad weather features. The results of their development efforts are verified in extensive tests under laboratory conditions and around the globe. **The pre-series vehicles travel at least twice through each season, in both the northern and southern hemispheres of our planet.** Dust, ice, cold, heat and all other rigors included.

#Messenger of spring

#Chronicle of a club community

#The first Porsche Club was formed back in 1952 — the brand was just four years young and not even 2,000 units of the 356 model had been produced in two and a half years of production in Stuttgart. In the beginning it was an association of just 13 Porsche drivers, which today has grown to over 180,000 members organized in Porsche Clubs worldwide. **As a tribute to the 13 club founders, 60 years later Porsche produced a small series of the 911 Club Coupé, limited to 13 units.** It was based on a Carrera S with a factory power output upgrade (430 hp instead of 400) and wore dark green, a rear spoiler in the ducktail shape and 20-inch aluminum rims over the ceramic brake system. The price was EUR 142,831. **But it could only be bought by Porsche Club members who apply online and are lucky enough to win the chance to purchase this anniversary piece.** Only customers in China and India were excluded from the drawing for legal reasons. Porsche combined the numerous activities of the clubs, which organize interesting events worldwide, from meetings to racing activities. One of the most popular major events is the "Rennsport Reunion" in Laguna Seca, California, where Porsche attractions come together both on and off the racetrack. Year after year, the Oldtimer Grand Prix at the Nürburgring also provides an interesting setting for Porsche owners and enthusiasts.

The fans and clubs are of great importance to the sports car manufacturer itself. 1980s-era Porsche CEO Peter Schutz summed it up thus: **"The customer always says what he thinks. You just have to keep your ear close enough to his mouth."** Accordingly, the company continues to this day to value closeness to the customer. Everywhere in the world and at every opportunity that presents itself. Or that can be created.

Moss Green Metallic

Porsche 911 Club Coupé (991/I), 2012
Minimax; Tibidabo

Porsche 911 Carrera “50 Years of 911” (991/1), 2013
Atlas; Bensberg

Dark Grey

#Anniversary pieces have a long tradition at Porsche. They are highly prized by media and customers alike. They offer the media a welcome opportunity to dedicate extensive coverage to the anniversary celebrations. And buyers can usually look forward to an above-average increase in value, after a phase of using the car. **Following the "30-year" 964 and "40-year" 996, a specially configured 991 played the role of the "50-year" 911.** Customers had a choice of three colors: Black, Geyser Gray Metallic and Graphite Gray. The first color is self-explanatory; the other two are reminiscent of the champagne yellow of the first 901 and the slate gray Hollywood star Steve McQueen preferred for his Porsche 911 — in a modern interpretation, of course, and in a contemporary glimmering metallic. The Pepita fabric on the seat panels was another reminder of the classic past. The first 911s were delivered with it...

The star-shaped 20-inch alloy wheels with brightly turned spokes, which are reminiscent of the two-tone Fuchs rims of the first and second generations of the 911, are also a reference to past style. Under the hood of the anniversary piece with the wide rear of the all-wheel drive Carrera is a 3.8-liter 400 hp engine. **Above it there was a trunk lid with a shining chrome horizontal ventilation grille, again reminiscent of the early 911.** The 911-50 (as shown on the logo) features a further air outlet with two decorative bars where the red strip of light was mounted on the all-wheel-drive vehicle. The premiere year of 1963 also specified the number of pieces, since the special model remained limited to 1,963 units. Even the confident price does not detract from the desirability. The cost of the birthday child, capable of 300 km/h and of sprinting from a standing start to 100 km/h in 4.5 seconds, is EUR 121,119.

#One more birthday child

#The product managers around August Achleitner once again put "the best 911 of all time" on wheels. This was how the Austrian was quoted by many journalists. And indeed, "Der Spiegel" also decreed that the 911 turbo S had redefined the limits of what was possible in a sports car suitable for daily use. This was made possible by, among other things, the new rear axle steering of the all-wheel sports car. **That made the car even more agile when cornering and also improved directional stability.** Depending on the speed, steering angle and driving situation, the rear wheels can steer or countersteer with an angle of up to 2.8 degrees. In addition, the variable front and rear spoilers can be adjusted in three stages. Shock absorbers and a new roll stabilizer are also electronically controlled and variable. In Porsche-speak, these technical attributes are known by the acronyms PASM (Porsche Active Suspension Management) and PDCC (Porsche Dynamic Chassis Control).

The usual plus in terms of power output that distinguishes the S from the "basic model" was considered a given. The 911 turbo delivers 520 hp; the turbo S, 560 hp. Starting in 2016, that increased further to 580 hp. When the turbo S was presented for model year 2014, more than EUR 30,000 separated it from the basic model. At EUR 195,256, it was just below the EUR 200,000 mark, which could easily be exceeded with a few extras. And all the more so when extravagant requests were desired, which the Porsche Exclusive Manufaktur knows very well how to bring to the street.

#Redefining the possibilities

White

911 turbo S (991/I), 2013
Minichamps; Paris

#Ultimate enjoyment, diet included

#The continuous strip of lights at the rear had meanwhile become an established style element for the all-wheel drive version of the 911 with its wider fenders, which has completed its seventh generation of 911 since 2012. And the targa — the body variant presented at the Detroit Motor Show in January 2014 and positioned between the Coupé and Cabriolet — was available exclusively with all-wheel drive. This had less to do with the fact that the semi-open body variant weighed 110 kg more than the Coupé than with the fact that targa customers prefer well-equipped vehicles and that comfort was more important than pure sportiness.

Despite equally notable design modifications to the body structure, the weight of the Cabriolet was ten kilos less than that of the targa, with its large rear window, below which the central roof section disappears (when open). The way in which the roll bar and rear window open to virtually devour the central part of the roof is a spectacle in itself. It takes just under 20 seconds.

But whether a Cabriolet or a Targa: Weight was always an issue on which Porsche engineers focused utmost attention. Or put more precisely, the reduction and avoidance of weight. Porsche's efforts in the design and production of the 911 are correspondingly great. **For example, large parts of the body, including the vehicle floor, are made of aluminum.** High-strength and ultra-high-strength steels are used at the critical points for safety and stiffness. After all, lightweight construction only becomes intelligent when the right material has been used at the right point on the vehicle. In concrete terms, this means that the 911 targa 4 has an unladen weight of 1,570 kg — putting it on a par with the VW Touran or BMW X1, which have much less powerful engines and are much less dynamic.

Sapphire Blue Metallic

Porsche 911 Carrera 4 targa (991/I), 2014
Minichamps; Paris

#The most powerful comes last

#In 2014 Porsche released the most powerful version of the "normal" 911 — the GTS — in the traditional manner, at an advanced stage of the model cycle. It delivered 430 hp and 50 Nm more torque than the hardly underpowered Carrera S. Larger brakes, a modified exhaust system and an extended Sport Chrono package with manually selectable driving programs were further amenities of the top model within the Carrera family. **The driving dynamics control came directly from the 918 Hybrid Spyder super sports car** and could be adjusted four ways — from Normal and Sport to Sport Plus and the Individual program. Also new was a feature called "Sport Response." It was part of the PDK transmission and released the maximum power output of the drive system for 20 seconds — an injection of power at the touch of a button. **Launch Control for best possible acceleration maneuvers was also included — if the optional PDK was installed.** Both the rear-wheel and all-wheel drive GTS have the wider rear end. As a targa, the GTS (EUR 146,228) also has a price gap of a good EUR 20,000 separate it from the rear-drive 911 Carrera GTS.

The type designation applied to the doors appears for the first time on the GTS of the 997 generation, and has already become a tradition on the 991. For the 991 it was still made of adhesive film, from the 992 generation onwards it could also be printed. Speaking of generational change: At the career end of the seventh generation, Porsche brought out the GTS version of the 991/II, based on the 3.0-liter twin turbo with powerful 450 hp and 550 Nm torque. Customarily strong were its striking appearance with standard 20-inch wheels painted in black and standard delivery with all the equipment items that support driving dynamics, which otherwise leaves 911 customers spoiled for choice with a view to the long list of possible equipment details.

With the GTS, 305 tires guaranteed sure road grip. Drivers of the rear-wheel drive vehicle usually get along well with those. The brake system with 6-piston calipers at the front and 4-piston calipers at the rear, which bite impressively and unyieldingly into pizza-sized brake discs, guaranteed the tightest braking distances even from high speeds. And the GTS as standard was fast: **The 420 hp model of the first series ran at a smooth 306 km/h, while the 450 hp variant accelerated to 312 km/h.**

GT Silver Metallic

Porsche 911 Carrera GTS (991/I), 2014
Schuco; Brooklyn Red Hook

Porsche 911 GT3 RS (997/I), 2015
Minichamps; New York

Lizard Green

#The GT3 in general, and the GT3 RS in particular, have firmly established themselves as the representatives of the "purity doctrine" for sports drivers and sports drivers with motorsport ambitions. **Purebred — this term absolutely does justice to the naturally aspirated racers with razor-sharp handling characteristics.** The RS version, which was noticeably more powerful than the GT3, appeared for the first time at the Geneva Salon in spring 2015, and would be sold from May onwards, at a starting price of EUR 181,690. In return, customers received a 4-liter engine with 500 hp and a 7-speed PDK. The nominal speed was 8,250 rpm, the maximum torque of 460 Nm reached already at 6,250 rpm. The scale showed 1,420 kg

While the classic GT3 presented itself with a Carrera-slim body, the RS was given the wide hips of the turbo. The sports cars — like all 911s — were manufactured in Stuttgart-Zuffenhausen. At Porsche's main plant, even the Cup vehicles (for worldwide motorsport competition) ran through production in harmony with the sports car siblings of the 718 and 911 families.

The slender 991 GT3 was already in its second model year at the time of the RS premiere. With a weight of 1,350 kg, it was the lightest GT3 of all ggenerations and had its origins in the 996 of 1999. Compared to the 997 GT3, the 991 was more powerful but at the same time also more economical — in the early years of the brand, Porsche development managers had already included the dictate in the specifications that every increase in performance must go hand in hand with lower fuel consumption. And the sports car manufacturer once again solved the task in a creditable manner, with *Top Gear* (a worldwide institution among the automotive media) awarding Porsche the "Engine of the Year" seal of approval for the GT3's propellant.

PDK was, incidentally, the standard transmission. And the rear-axle steering, presented for the first time in the turbo, was noticeably beneficial for the handling of the car. Starting with the facelift of the 991, the GT3 — also as a reaction to the big response to the limited 911 R — was available again with a manual transmission.

#Purebred

Porsche 911 Carrera (991/II), 2015
Herpa; Stuttgart-Zuffenhausen

Slate Grey

#Turbo for all

#Porsche presented the 2016 model year at the IAA 2015. **The aspirated engine become obsolete for emissions protection reasons: from now on they were all Carrera and Carrera S turbos.** However, this alone does not do justice to the new model. As was practically a tradition, presentation of the new 911 was met by an outcry from the fan community. But just as traditionally, that calmed down again quite quickly. The second series of the seventh generation 911 gets a new heart — that is, a new 3.0-liter (2,981 cc) engine with two turbochargers and charge-air cooling. An additional 20 hp compared to the predecessor models had a soothing effect. The engine torque increased by a full 60 Newton meters to 450 Nm and 500 Nm, respectively. The 50 hp difference between the power output in the Carrera and the Carrera S arises in the periphery of the twin turbo 3.0-liter engine — that is, due to differently dimensioned compressors and charging pressures. In its base version, the Carrera delivers 370 hp.

The standard scope of delivery now includes an even more powerful Porsche Active Suspension Management (PASM) including a chassis lowered by 10 millimeters. Externally, the new model can be identified by a revamped front apron, three-dimensionally profiled taillights, and the black, ribbed radiator grille on the hood. **Customers also valued the enhanced infotainment system with smartphone integration, 7-inch touchscreen and state-of-the-art online navigation.** At Porsche, this was referred to as Porsche Communication Management, or PCM for short, and was gradually being enriched with ever-more extensive applications and service offerings.

#A sustainable automobile — maybe even the most sustainable

#The 3.0-liter twin turbo Carrera S is sustainably powered by 420 hp. **Experienced drivers lapped the legendary Nürburgring Nordschleife with this in 7:30 — 10 seconds faster than with the predecessor model.** This was due not only to the increased engine power but also to the rear-axle steering, which is now also available in the Carrera S. The new Carrera S is also equipped with a rear-axle steering system. That was previously reserved for the GT3 and turbo. Especially on tracks like the demanding Nordschleife, the extra power conducive to driving dynamics can exploit its qualities. The new suspension tuning includes a further lowering by 10 millimeters.

Anyone not satisfied with what was actually quite decent performance could find what they were looking for in the price list: The item "Performance increase Carrera S" could be found under the abbreviation X51. This meant a de facto 450 hp, a top speed of up to 313 km/h (Carrera S) and acceleration to 100 in, at best (Carrera 4S), 4.0 seconds, or to 200 in 13.1 seconds. In addition to a sports exhaust system and the Sport Chrono package with dynamic engine mounts and modified brake cooling, the scope of delivery also includes larger exhaust turbochargers. The surcharge for this was a good EUR 10,000. Fifteen years earlier, 450 hp was also the power rating for the performance-enhanced Porsche 996 turbo ex works, which also produced 420 hp as standard.

One of the most popular extras was the PDK transmission. PDK stands for the "Porsche Doppel-Kupplung" (Porsche dual-clutch) transmission and appeared as an abbreviation for the first time in motorsports in the mid-1980s. In parallel to Audi, which was trying to develop PDK to serial-production maturity in the World Rally Championship Group B Sport quattro racers, Porsche was working with the Group C 962 racing car. Walter Röhrl and Hans-Joachim Stuck are their most prominent test and development drivers. This efficient and lightning-fast shifting technology experienced its breakthrough in series production with Porsche with the facelift of the 997 model series. The 7-speed PDK could be shifted manually — as is customary in racing — using shift paddles on the steering wheel — or can be driven in automatic mode. A coasting function — in conjunction with engine start-stop — was one of the details of the modern 3.0-liter twin turbo, which was fully trimmed for efficiency and environmental friendliness. Around 90 percent of all 911 customers were willing to pay an extra EUR 3,500 for this.

Porsche also offered a number of other options that proved beneficial to the driving dynamics. These included, for example, Porsche Torque Vectoring, in which differential lock as well as precise braking impulses impressively influence the cornering steering behavior of the vehicle, sport suspension, dynamic chassis control with electromechanical roll stabilizer, and the previously mentioned rear-axle steering. **In addition, with the Porsche Ceramic Composite Brake, there are the already well-known upgrades to the brake system.**

That the 911 has developed into what is likely the most timeless automobile in history is certainly also thanks to the constant attention to detail and the continuous development and refinement of the iconic sports car's finesse and performance. This is evidenced not only by the regular awards in reader surveys such as that of the industry magazine *auto, motor und sport*. For decades, the Porsche 911 has been and remains at the lonely top here.

White

Porsche 911 Carrera 4S (991/II), 2016
Herpa; Berlin

#Matters of course

#Porsche entered the 2014 Endurance World Championship and returned to Le Mans, or as Porsche sometimes describes it, the brand's "living room." And it did so in the top category known as LMP1, in which Audi, Toyota and Porsche compete with hi-tech hybrid prototypes. **For the dark hours of the night, even if they are short in summer, brilliant light is part of the package of tasks for the racing car developers.** Accordingly, four laser lights flood the darkness of central France with glaring light from the 919 hybrid — that's the name of the hi-tech spacecraft. From this point on, these four points would also become the distinguishing features of the two- and four-door sports cars from Stuttgart on the roads of the world. While the light units of the 919 hybrid turn night into day and light the way to six World Championship titles and three Le Mans victories for the factory drivers, the four LED light points appearing from model year 2015 serve as the daytime running lights long prescribed in Europe.

A small matter and hardly worth mentioning — after all, the pure, always attractive shape of the 911 is enough of a distinguishing feature. Self-explanatory, so to speak. And yet it is sometimes also necessary to repeat self-evident facts. Porsche CEO Oliver Blume once again gets to the heart of the matter: "A real Porsche must be authentic. It must give its driver the feeling of confidence in all situations. The most important parameters for me are the drive system, chassis, steering and brakes, which make possible the highest possible safety and vehicle control. **A Porsche offers a fascinating, emotional and sporty driving experience." Nothing more needs to be said.**

White

Porsche 911 turbo Cabriolet (991/II), 2016
Herpa; Veilbronn

Porsche 911 R (991/II), 2016
Minimax; Berlin

Black

#The magic of doing without

#At Porsche, R stands for racing. And for two outstanding lightweights in the model history of the 911. The initial impetus for the 911 came from Porsche nephew Ferdinand Piëch, who, as head of development from 1965 onwards, shared responsibility for the fate of the then-family-owned company. His first project was finished in 1967. Together with Rolf Wütherich — the passenger in James Dean's fatal drive in the 550 Spyder in 1955 — he rigorously slimmed down the 911 and rid it of all unnecessary ingredients. Fenders, hoods and doors are made of plastic, the glazing is Plexiglas, pull straps are used instead of door handles, small lamps instead of standard rear lights. Wherever possible, plates and components are made lighter with holes. The list of weight-loss measures is long. And in the end, the 1,030 kg of a standard 911 S became just 800 kg. Never had there been a lighter 911. And as if that weren't enough, the racing 911 underwent an output enhancement in the form of a 210 hp 6-cylinder heart implant into the 906 racing sports car.

Five decades after the birth of the original 911 R, Porsche was recalling its history once again: A new 911 R was available in Geneva at the beginning of 2016, this time naturally based on the 991 series. It was the vanguard of a small series limited to 991 units. And with a dry weight of 1,250 kilograms (the empty weight is 1,370 kg), it was again the lightest 911 of its generation. The key to happiness once again lay in doing without: No insulation material, no PDK transmission, no leather, no cage and no spoiler. In addition, there was the high-torque 4-liter 6-cylinder engine with 460 Nm and 500 hp, well-known from the GT3. Other ingredients, such as the chassis, also came from that model. And, as with his predecessors, the youngest 911 R also required one to dig deep into their pockets as Porsche wanted EUR 189,544 for the car. But that didn't scare the crowd of enthusiasts at all as the 323 km/h top model was sold out even before its exhibition premiere. Even the LMP1 drivers lost out, and neither the factory nor the dealers were able to obtain one of the models, which represented a considerable investment from the very first day.

And for those who couldn't get their hands on a 911 R at all, Porsche offered an almost unlimited 911 R with the 911 GT3 Touring presented at the IAA 2017; a GT3 without wing mechanism and roll cage but with numerous possibilities to customize the minimalist, likewise manual transmission 4-liter 500 hp sports car according to one's own tastes and preferences. Starting price: EUR 152,460.

Porsche 911 Carrera S (991/II), 2017
Minimax; Herzogenaurach

Irish Green

#For its anniversary, Porsche presented itself with a 911 Carrera S in Irish green. The performance-enhanced 3-liter twin turbo engine of the Coupé assembled on May 11, 2017, delivered 450 hp. Its individual equipment advertises the "Exclusive Manufaktur" with which Porsche is always capable of responding to unusual customer requests. As with the special "911-50" model launched four years earlier to mark the 50th birthday of the 911, the color and interior design are reminiscent of the roots of the iconic series. **The dark green had been the favorite color of company founder Ferry Porsche, who preferred this shade for his company cars.** Inside, the seat panels were covered with black and white houndstooth fabric. Incidentally, Irish Green has been one of the special colors in which the 911 could be ordered since 1965; for decades now, customers have also been able to order.

The 911 has developed splendidly in the eight generations from the 901 to the 911 — including the models with safety bumpers, which are often referred to (not quite correctly) as the "G series" — 964, 993, 996, 997, 991 and up to the recently introduced 992. The current 911 consistently demonstrates the apex of what is possible and thus remains true to itself. Only 82 vehicles of the 901 were produced before Ferry Porsche unbureaucratically declared it the 911. Between 1964 and 1973, Porsche produced 81,100 first-generation 911 vehicles in Stuttgart-Zuffenhausen. The second generation of the 911 (with bellows bumpers and rear strip of lights), manufactured from autumn 1973 to 1989, produced 198,414 vehicles. Porsche produced 74,008 units of the 964 generation, which began production at the same time; its successor, the last air-cooled 993 generation, resulted in another in 67,535 units.

The fifth generation of the 911, the 996, represented a paradigm shift as water cooling was introduced into the 911 in 1997. It found 179,163 enthusiastic buyers. The controversial front headlamp was eliminated from its successor, the 997 generation, which was manufactured 215,092 times. The 991 series, produced in Zuffenhausen between 2011 and 2019, is set to once again surpass this figure.

Porsche manufactured 32,994 units of the 4-cylinder 912, primarily for the US market. In 2017, the 370 hp 911 Carrera was priced at EUR 97,914. This was about four times the price of a VW Golf 1.4 TSI Comfortline. When the 130 hp ancestor of the 1965 911 was delivered, Porsche charged a mere DM 21,900. The middle class reference car of those days — a VW 1300 Export — also cost one fourth the price of the 6-cylinder sports car. The highest price to date for a used 911 was a staggering **EUR 1.76 million. This was fetched at a 2015 auction in Pebble Beach by a 911 turbo 3.0 that had been the property of Steve McQueen.** The likewise Slate Gray 911 S, which was purchased and used by Steve McQueen in 1970 for shooting the film *Le Mans*, brought USD 1.375 million at a 2011 auction in neighboring Monterey.

#The millionaire

#Lot size: one

#The cost of a 991 turbo S in 2017 was EUR 205,000. The turbo S fulfills the wishes of most sports car fans in standard trim, but Porsche traditionally knows how to fulfill individual wishes as well. Therefore Porsche presented the 911 turbo S Exclusive Series, preassembled in three eye-catching colors, loaded with luxurious accessories and limited to 500 units. The unit price for the showpiece available in Agate Gray Metallic, Carrera White Metallic or Golden Yellow Metallic with roof, hood, spoiler and side skirts made of carbon: EUR 259,992. **Finishing has a long tradition at Porsche, as the Stuttgart-based company has known from the outset how to respond to special customer requests.** Whereas details used to be discussed between salespeople and customers — whether it was for a paint job in the same color as a tie, a performance boost or even the realization of a street-legal 935 — now, the sports car manufacturer offers the Exclusive range. The go-ahead was given in 1986 for the "Exclusive Manufaktur" located in Zuffenhausen's Plant 1 (alongside the CEO and Communications). This is where all (well, almost all) customer wishes are turned into reality. **Not only in small series but also from "lot sizes of one" — that is, unique specimens.**

In the case of the golden turbo S Exclusive Series presented in Goodwood 2017, the visual measures are complemented by a subtle increase in performance from 580 to 608 hp. With this the all-wheel drive car stormed from a standing start to country road speed in 2.9 seconds and reached 200 km/h within 9.6 seconds. At 330, the drive to accelerate balances out driving resistances.

Incidentally, that same year one of the 280 km/h 964 turbo S Lightweight cars changed hands at an auction in Silverstone for EUR 668,000. And the golden-yellow 991 would serve as a model for a special 911 turbo built by the specialists at Porsche Exclusive Manufaktur for the 70th anniversary in 2018. Twenty years after production of the 993 generation ended, a one-off piece built on a body-in-white in stock and with over 6,500 original parts from the Porsche Classic collection changed hands in late 2018 for EUR 2.7 million. Proceeds from the auction will go to projects of the non-profit Ferry Porsche Foundation. Porsche enthusiasts from all over the world benefit from the extensive spare parts pool of the specialists at Porsche Classic.

Golden Yellow Metallic

Porsche 911 turbo S “Exclusive Series“ (991/II), 2017
Minimax; Manhattan

#Diabolo 911

#The original 911 turbo is regarded with respect and awe as a wild creature that only experienced masters can tame and control in road traffic. The delayed, enormous thrust that deploys in combination with rear-wheel drive — and the lack of all assistance systems that now make even the most powerfully motorized automobiles drivable — are the stuff of legends. This came to an end with the 993 generation of the 911, since the most powerful 911 in this series comes with ABS and all-wheel drive. For homologation for racing use, Porsche began producing the GT2, which had to dispense with four-wheel drive to ensure a level competitive playing field on the racetrack. So much for the Genesis of the GT2, which has long since been replaced on the track by the 911 GT3 Cup and RSR models as well as the Cayman GT4. But as the wildest of all 911s, it still has a following today. The most powerful of all 911s mobilizes 700 hp and a brutish 750 Nm of torque from its twin-turbocharged 3.8-liter heart. Compared to its predecessor, this means: more power, more carbon, more titanium, larger turbochargers, less weight. GT2 RS needs just 2.8 seconds to complete a Formula One-worthy sprint to 100 km/h. And with a top speed of 340 km/h, it is also the fastest of all 911s. **The British cult car magazine *Top Gear* awarded the GT2 RS the "Code Brown Award for Scariest Device of the Year."** The diabolic nature of this driving machine also fit with the standard bright red Alcantara roof liner. In sum, the 911 GT2 RS was a package that even race drivers dream of.

The 911 GT2 RS experienced its trial by fire in 2017 at the Festival of Speed, the aristocratic motorsport event held every summer on the Goodwood Estate of the Lord of March — or as he is known by his full name: Charles Henry Gordon-Lennox, 11th Duke of Richmond, 11th Duke of Lennox, 11th Duke of Aubigny, 6th Duke of Gordon. With 7-speed PDK and shift paddles behind the black-and-red steering wheel with suede leather feel, the 340 km/h two-seater would make its exhibition debut at the IAA. And a short time later, it ennobled itself with a fabulous time of 6:47.3 minutes for a lap around the Nürburgring Nordschleife.

The supercar weighs 1,470 kilos with standard equipment. As before for the 918 hybrid, there is a Weissach package with which the weight can be reduced by 30 kilos for a surcharge of just under EUR 29,750 on the base price of EUR 285,220.

Miami Blue

Porsche 911 GT2 RS (991), 2017
Minimax; Brooklyn

Porsche 911 GT3 Touring (991/II), 2017
Minimax; Brooklyn

Lava Orange

#The wolf in sheep's clothing

#Also at the IAA 2017, Porsche presented the Touring Package for the GT3, another nuance in the wide range of 911 models. With this the sports car manufacturer is targeting **"lovers of top-class sports cars with a pronounced penchant for understatement and classic driving pleasure."** The Touring version of the GT3 dispenses with the striking rear wing mechanism of the original model without increasing or decreasing the price of over EUR 150,000. In the interior, luxurious leather took precedence over non-slip Alcantara. In addition, there was a manual 6-speed transmission with a dual-mass flywheel for added comfort. The 7-speed dual-clutch transmission was also available at no extra charge. In essence, the GT3 Touring is the legitimate — and unlimited — successor to the swiftly soldout 911 R. A 911 R for everyone, so to speak. The 4-liter boxer with its huge displacement is the last aspirated engine in the lineup; all other 911 engines are now turbocharged. 500 horsepower and a remarkable torque of 460 Newton meters mistreat the powered rear wheels, which demonstrate above-average grip behavior — thanks to rear-axle steering; dynamic engine mounts; Porsche Traction Management (PTM); the ingenious Porsche Active Suspension (PASM) driving dynamics program, which can be controlled in several stages; Porsche Stability Management (PSM); Porsche Torque Vectoring (PTV); and rear differential lock with asymmetrical locking. With the GT3, the engineers developed the systems and their interaction with the steering, gas pedal and brake to a level of perfection that left nothing for driving dynamics experts to desire. Whether on the circuit, the country road or the long tour. **The designation Touring Package was a clear reference to the equipment version formerly available for the Carrera RS 2.7.** With the GT3 Touring, Porsche has successfully transported this concept into modern times. And if you like, you can travel up to 316 km/h in this top-class Gran Turismo. With standard equipment.

Porsche 911 Carrera T (991/II), 2017
Herpa; Venice Beach

Rhodium Silver Metallic

#Unfiltered and pure

#In parallel to the Touring package for the GT3, Porsche presented the 911 Carrera T. It was essentially a harmoniously assembled variant based on the basic 911, with the addition of all the technology options beneficial to driving dynamics (including rear-axle steering — not usually not available in the 911 Carrera) but dispensing with equipment details that added unwanted comfort and weight. In addition, there are pull straps instead of door handles and lightweight glass, as is not otherwise provided for in the surcharge list for the 911 of the seventh generation. The car can be ordered with a standard 7-speed manual transmission. **In addition, the 911 T has no air conditioning, navigation system or rear seat system.** These features may, however, be ordered back in the car at no extra cost. "The unfiltered truth" is how the marketing specialists defined the model T of the 911, which can be identified from the outside by its rims, mirror caps and a decorative strip on the side in Agate Gray. With 370 hp, it is not one of the most powerful, but with a weight-optimized Sport Chrono package including a chassis that is 20 millimeters lower, shorter shift distance and a specially designed interior with a mix of fabric and Alcantara, it is one of the most prominent members of the family. **The weight-loss program for the 911 T resulted in an overall weight reduction of 20 kg.**

#The 2018 expansion stage of the late-era 991-based model 911 GT3 mobilizes 520 hp. And as an RS, it does justice to the reference to racing in its name. The 911 GT3 RS comes as standard with a wide range of aerodynamic add-ons at the front and rear, a 7-speed PDK transmission, rear-axle steering and a robust ceramic brake system with generous 380 mm discs at the front axle. **These don't just slow the sports car down — they virtually nail it to the asphalt. The braking distance from 100 km/h is 32.9 meters.** And the 911 GT3 RS, accelerated from a standstill, achieves that speed in just 3.2 seconds. The 200 km/h mark is reached in 10.8 seconds, and 250 km/h is reached in 18.8 seconds. The maximum speed is 312 km/h. This means that the 911 GT3 RS is hardly the top dog in head-to-head comparison — against a GT2 RS, for example — but on the circuit, hardly another sports car can match its courage.

The quick revving of the 3,996 cc 6-cylinder boxer is seductive. Its rated power is 8,250 rpm, and the shift command is issued at 9,000 rpm. The car is personalized self-confidence. As is its price, unfortunately, which is EUR 195,137.

But it's also possible to be even more self-confident: For those who want to add a bit more flourish, Porsche offers a Weissach package — just as with the 918 hybrid Spyder and 911 GT2 RS. This includes, for a surcharge of EUR 17,850, a weight reduction of 18 kg compared to the model with Clubsport equipment. Among other things, it includes a carbon hood, roof and stabilizers, magnesium rims, lightweight plastic discs and a titanium roll bar instead of the steel one in the standard sibling model. A further EUR 3,570 surcharge will get you the special color "Chalk," which follows the previously extremely popular "Slate Gray" as a special trend color.

Like many Porsche models before it, this 911 will also be fine-tuned with the assistance of Porsche representative Walter Röhrl. The two-time World Rally Champion, the "ultimate authority in driving dynamics," is also regarded as a master of catchy slogans: "A garage without a Porsche 911 is just a bleak and empty hole." There's not really much we could add to that.

#Ultralight heavyweight

Chalk

Porsche 911 GT3 RS Weissach Package (991/II), 2018
Minichamps; Schlosshotel Elmau

Porsche 911 Carrera S (991/I), 2011

Porsche 911 Carrera S Cabriolet (991/I), 2012

Porsche 911 Carrera S Cabriolet (991/I), 2012

Porsche 911 Carrera Club Coupé (991/I), 2012

Porsche 911 Carrera "50 years 911" (997/I), 2013

Porsche 911 turbo S (991/I), 2013

Porsche 911 Carrera 4 targa (991/I), 2014

Porsche 911 Carrera GTS (991/I), 2014

Porsche 911 GT3 RS (997/I), 2015

Porsche 911 Carrera (991/II), 2015

911 Carrera 4S (997/II), 2016

Porsche 911 turbo Cabriolet (991/II), 2016

#Generation VII (991)

Porsche 911 R, 2016

Porsche 911 Carrera S (991/II), 2017

Porsche 911 turbo S Exclusive Series (991/II), 2017

Porsche 911 GT2 RS (991), 2017

Porsche 911 GT3 Touring (991/II), 2017

Porsche 911 GT3 RS Weissach-Paket (991/II), 2018

Gentian Blue Metallic

#Generation VIII

(992)

#Next generation

With concise tweaks on the trunk lid, an excitingly elongated flank and a narrow strip of LED lights at the rear, the eighth generation of the 911 family speaks a contemporary language of form and yet is the same as it ever was. A typical 911, that is. **And when extended, the rear spoiler is reminiscent of the tail unit that kept the 959 on course even at top speed.** But with 450 hp from the 3-liter Carrera S, the 2019 model of the 911 year falls precisely within the territory formerly reserved for the 959 supercar. Under its outer shell now completely made from aluminum, the eighth generation of the 911 shows off new features. On the interior, the large displays are immediately noticeable. In addition, there are new assistance systems like wet mode, in which the vehicle acoustically detects wet road surfaces and adapts the vehicle accordingly.

The first 992 rolled off the assembly line in the summer, and in late November 2018, the curtain opened for the — once again — best 911 of all time at the Los Angeles Auto Show. It is the last 911 created under the authority of "Gustl" Achleitner. Just in time for the presentation of the 992, he passed the baton to Frank-Steffen Walliser in Weissach, who had previously been responsible for GT motorsport for Porsche and made vehicles such as the 918 hybrid Spyder, the 911 RSR and the 935 a reality.

Meanwhile the chassis construction moved into new buildings in Zuffenhausen. The last production plant is thus clearing out of the "shed roof" halls in Plant 2 that were steeped in tradition. Production of the 356 began in the 1950s in these halls, thus paving the way that the 911 has traveled up to today.
The premiere of the latest 911 comes at a time when Porsche is investing massively in the future. **In parallel to further development of the sports car icon, the company is shaping the future of the sports car in the form of the all-electric Taycan.** New production facilities are being built for this in Stuttgart-Zuffenhausen — while the 911 is being manufactured in previously unattainable quantities. As they say at Porsche, fittingly: "Only those who continuously reinvent themselves can still be themselves tomorrow." This applies to the 911 in particular and the Porsche brand in general...

CEO Oliver Blume summarizes it as follows: "There is probably no other automobile that has been so consistently adapted to the demands of a modern sports car and has remained so unmistakably true to its external and internal values as the 911. The Porsche 911 is in principle always the same sports car, despite our uncompromising commitment to progress. And the same goes for our company."

Lava Orange

Porsche 911 Carrera S (992), 2019
Maisto; LA Convention Center

Generation VIII (992)

Dolomite Silver Metallic

Porsche 911 Carrera S (992), 2019

#Snap-shots of another dimension

#About the author and the idea

#Toy cars have been a part of Jörg Walz's life since he was a small boy, with automotive media coming along during his school days and, several years ago, photography as well. Over the past decades the author has had the pleasure of experiencing and reporting on the history of the automobile and automotive racing from up close — as an editor for various trade media and as a communicator in the automotive industry.

The photos in this book were actually the content of a spontaneous social media project that long ago developed into a full-fledged passion. As a result, shots originally taken for a short-term Instagram series have grown into a well-stocked digital automotive museum. The distinctive photos have meanwhile been supplemented in analog form with book publications and their own art exhibit (in the Nuremberg gallery "VON&VON").

Their special appeal lies in the interplay between the miniature cars and their real-world surroundings. This is able to portray the history of the originals, as well as capturing a few surprised smiles. The photos provide new perspectives.

Everything — the model car and the background — is familiar and yet somehow alien. And the settings all over the world invite the viewer to travel along in their minds. The spontaneously staged photos have also encouraged imitators — since all of the photos are simply "iPhoneographed", without the use of extra tools or artificial arrangements.